MW00913826

CONTENTS

THE SITUATION WE FACE & A SUMMARY VISION

Trump's approach will lead to a dictatorship, not power to the people as he claims. The best approach to defeating Trump is to go in the other direction, and propose a strategy that will positively strengthen everything that has provided greater democracy, strength, peace, and economic growth – reinforcing it with a strong emphasis on Jobs and Economy (methodically, in a fair, innovative and sustainable way - that also increases the wealth and assets at the bottom of the economic ladder) aimed at weaning away those Trump supporters who voted for him on this basis. Trump's claims that the economy is doing better under him are false – the economy was doing better already thanks to Obama, where we went from losing about 800,000 jobs per month to steady job growth, recovery from a financial crisis (which Trump will again cause), an infrastructure investment that helped the economy, an unemployment rate that went down to about 5%, and many quarters in which the economy grew at a high rate and the stock market did well.

Rather than giving power back to the people, Trump is leading like a dictator, by weakening democracy. There are significant efforts to strengthen democracy - these are the fight for voter rights, eliminating gerrymandering, and complete campaign finance reform. These must be strengthened in every way and go beyond just counteracting his efforts and those of the Republicans.

To this we have to add a courageous approach that portrays and strengthens positive trends, gets more power to the people, strengthens the nation by strengthening diversity, discourages violent language and behavior, strengthens freedom of speech and the press, ends discrimination and harassment of women and minorities and strengthens women's rights, suppresses destructive mass militaristic mobilization, and provides more and better jobs and economy in a way that's better for all and for environment and our planet Earth!

Our nation faces historical challenges that will determine whether our future is good politically, socially, financially, environmentally, and militarily – with, peace, prosperity, idealism and security, or whether we do into sudden or steady decline – the end of the American era. It will also determine whether the increasing inequality of income can be reversed and whether those at lower end of the income and asset scale will get the minimum needed for their basic needs and for enjoying sustainable livelihoods. What we do now is therefore super important.

Highlights of the Situation We Face

- All of our democratic institutions are under attack and are being weakened by irresponsible behavior by Trump and the Republicans

- Imperfections and abuses were there before Trump came, but instead of reforming the democratic system, we have gone from the frying pan into the fire.
- Tax cuts for the wealthy are not spurring job growth or revival of manufacturing jobs
- The Defense Budget is being increased way beyond what is needed and strategy with our allies or globally is leading to instability and scorn for the USA – opposite of what Trump claims.
- Big increases in the Federal Deficit are being caused by Tax cuts and increased Defense spending
- Tariffs imposed are hurting farmers, consumers, and our allies, while not sufficiently addressing the true trade reforms we need to lead to more good paying jobs.
- Externally, the US has withdrawn from its commitment to solve the climate change problem, and internally, it has directed the Environmental Protection Agency to allow commercial interests to start destroying and polluting the environment.
- The national leadership has encouraged bigotry, hatred and targeting minorities and political opposition that are dividing the nation, and even the white working class.
- Women's rights and the rights of minorities like blacks, tribal nations, minority religions, Latin-Americans and immigrants are under attack and are being made to feel inferior.
- Externally, Trump is ruining the relationships with all of our Allies, and encouraging Dictators like Kim and Putin, while discouraging our democratic allies and global democracy.
- Deregulation and a lack of policing of the financial sector (more than what happened under George Bush), has increased the danger of a financial crisis worse than 2008.
- Attacks on the rule of law and our primary institutions that maintain them – the FBI, the CIA and the Intelligence community are under attack. While the excesses of the past have to be curtailed, the damage being done to them and the rule of law is destructive.

A Summary Statement of Where We Should be Headed as a Nation

The major attempt of this book is to get Americans started on the path of an alternative vision, that they can refine as they go along. The vision that is presented here includes a stronger democracy, a much stronger jobs and economy strategy that is pro-employment and pro-environment, better universal healthcare, a better and more environmentally sustainable economy, more fulfilment of basic needs, stronger minority rights, an environmentally clean nation, stronger women's rights, considerably reduced internal violence, common sense gun control, a pro-employment and pro-environment trade strategy, reform of financial sectors so that they are more favorable for Main Street, and a sensible defense policy that does not break the bank and promotes both security and world peace. This book needs to be in the hand of everyone: movements leaders, party leaders, candidates, elected officials, organization leaders, people politically active, and then last but not least, all voters and all citizens. This manual and related book is intended to energize, educate, motivate and arm political activists, citizens and voters to turn their country around, so that America provides a fair prosperity to all in a manner that is good for itself and for the world.

What this book and the accompanying manual propose are alternative Visions of how this nation could be much better for all, including those who right now support Trump and the Republicans. The nation will be much better off if all people are included in the affairs and benefits of the nation, if all people were enabled to be more equal in every way, if the rich and powerful truly earn their incomes rather than steal and create crises and deny others and the communities their fair share of income and assets, if there are jobs and economy methods that empower all to participate in creating income and assets, if there is genuine security and justice for all, including minorities, if the military has sufficient strength without spending excessive amounts that bust the budget and balloon the deficit and cooperate with our allies in maintaining a fair and genuine world peace that encourages worldwide democracy, if the democracy that we have truly learns from the lessons of the past and the excesses of the Republicans to create an open, transparent and participatory democracy, and if the type of progress that we have is such that is good for planet Earth and all life on it, solves the big environmental problems like Climate Change and contribute to making our nation clean, beautiful, and naturally productive, with healthy and happy empowered people doing all of it! Quite a mouthful – but intended to be good for all!

Alternative Visions Proposed Herein - Summary Points

- We have to undo all of the damages that have been and are being done by highlighting the situation we face
- We need to learn from the past and the current devastation to **strengthen our Democracy** more than it has ever been. We need to give up the arrogance that our democracy is better than those of others, and proceed to reform and strengthen it to make it much better much more open, transparent and participatory, and truly empower people at all levels, while reforming the legislative, judicial, media, and executive branches of government so that people are truly empowered.
- **All citizens have to be first class citizens** regardless of race, color, national origin, gender, religion or sexual orientation – the needs of all have to be addressed. Our Diversity is our strength and must be strengthened further. Women's and minority rights have to be strengthened!
- **We must improve the quality of our nation by better healthcare, education and infrastructure – these investments are the most worthwhile of all!**
- The destructive aspects of our financial system that allow some people to benefit from insane profits while creating crises and poverty for the rest have to be replaced by a positive and constructive approach, where the financial

system behaves responsibly, serves the communities, nation, workers and farmers, and shares the benefits with the rest of the nation. Main street has to be empowered with a better Jobs and Economy strategy that enable all to earn their income and improve their assets by the nation implementing pro-employment, pro-environment and pro-asset generating strategies.

- Internally, the epidemic of gun violence has to solved by a combination of **gun control,** mental health, social and economic programs that make it less likely that individuals will behave violently and if they have violent intentions, that they cannot do much damage because they cannot access rapid fire type assault weapons.
- **Externally the nation has to have the combination of a strong defense policy** that works cooperatively with our allies, does not require an insanely high defense budget, and works globally towards a more peaceful and safer world.
- **Solutions to Climate Change and the global ecological crisis** (where we are destroying the life support systems of the planet) require ALL of the nations of the world to cooperate to make it happen. Even when we resume global leadership, we will need more effective global institutions, resources and strategies to solve these big problems. We have to stop having an abhorrence for global and United Stations type institutions, and instead work to build global institutions that are effective and empowered (even to supersede trade and financial rules, when needed) to make things happen.
- **Our nation has been a nation of immigrants.** While we must undo the damage done to our Tribal Nations brothers and sisters, even as we try to limit immigration, we must remain open to immigrants. An immigration policy is needed that is just, humane, compassionate, and serves the nation's interests.

Overview – The Past, the Present & the Future

For thousands of years, native American Tribes had lived in all of the Americas. European migration led to a reversal of the fortunes of native Americans, who suffered a great deal. Then slaves were imported from Africa that helped the agriculture to thrive, but was tragic for the African Americans. The US Constitution attempted to learn from other democratic systems, and solve the abuses of monarchies and religious persecution. Although initially only propertied white males could vote, this was later expanded to include all white males. Women had to fight for and finally earn the right to vote, but still continued to be treated unequally. African Americans, although freed from slavery by the American Civil War did not really get the right to vote till the 1960s after the civil rights movement, but still suffered discrimination. Then, after World War II, and especially after the Vietnam War, the US opened its door to migration of skilled people from all over the world. So today, while the white population (of European descent) dominates, the US is like a reflection of the whole world, with people from all over the world. The US derives much of its strength from its ability to command the loyalty of people of all colors, races, genders, religions, national origins and sexual orientations.

In parallel, after massive agricultural progress, fueled quite a bit by the availability of good agricultural land, but also in the early stages by the application of slaves, and later by the application of labor saving machinery. However, all was not well, and conservation practices and to be put in place to help the US recover from the Dust Bowl era of the 1920s and 1930s. Picking up from Great Britain, the US began in the nineteenth and early twentieth centuries to become a dominating force in the industrial revolution of the West. This industrialization enabled it to rapidly convert its industry at the start of World War II to armaments and war related production, in order to help the Allies defeat Hitler, Japan and the axis powers. By giving many safety net type economic benefits and depression era programs, it prevented the US from going to either the fascist or communist political extremes, although even Eisenhower warned of the dangers posed by the developed military-industrial complex. Although Europe, Japan and South-east Asia are still a significant forces, and China has come up as a major competitor, the US still remains the largest economy of the world.

Also, during its era of industrialization, the levels of air, water and soil pollution had reached very high levels. The toxic, hazardous and radioactive waste generated many "superfund sites" that needed to be cleaned up as they were poisoning the air, the water, and the land. The so called green agricultural revolution had meant the high use of poisonous pesticides and herbicides. All of these had led to high levels of pollution where the lakes, rivers, air and ground water were becoming unfit for people. It took many decades of the passing and implementation of the Clean Air Act and the Clean Water Act to clean up the waterways, air and land masses of the nations, although much of the toxic pollution remains at many sites. With its abandoning of these regulations, Trump is taking the nation backwards!

For a few decades after the war, the majority of people in the US shared in the new wealth being created with a thriving middle class receiving reasonably good pay and benefits, although much of this had often to be won by labor organizing and the union movement. Since then, the financial, corporate, political and international trade systems BY DESIGN have continued to create a massive inequality of wealth, with the large middle class almost disappearing. The selfish practices of the upper levels of society have continued to impoverish those at the lower levels, and financial and political power has continued to concentrate at upper levels. Global trade agreements have also been written to mainly benefit these larger US companies.

The current US political situation is such that Trump came along at a time when this dissatisfaction among most of the population had reached high levels, and has, with a false populism promised all kinds of benefits to these people, while the Democratic Party has not attempted to properly protect or rally the disadvantaged, and even the working-class folks and rural families. There were political abuses and lack of responsiveness, that he played upon. Also, he has tried to scapegoat immigrants, especially those from Mexico and Central America, arguing that they are taking over jobs and benefits, and tried to scapegoat immigrants from Islamic countries with the fears of terrorism. By the slogan "Make America Great Again", he has tried to provide a slogan and imagery that says that it wants to take America back to the past where there were high paying industrial jobs, and has also pandered to the sentiments of white supremacists.

The US, while doing well in terms of the total wealth, faces multiple crises, ecological, social, economic, healthcare wise and militarily. The nation needs an overarching vision that will help itself pull out of its inequality and morass. If the US transforms itself, only the US can provide the leadership to solve the problems of global warming, the global ecological crisis and help maintain peace and security if it changes its way of doing things.

What this Book and the accompanying Manual are attempting to do are to give America an alternative bold, courageous and uplifting vision to that of Trump which would inspire not only the Democratic Party, but also all of those movements who oppose Trump, and those who would like to be active – in short, inspire, energize and motivate, not only to vote, but also work hard to transform the society. There are those who started a resistance movement, which goes by the name of RESIST, and then along came the re-uniting movement that called itself INDIVISIBLE, with the Move On and the Progressive movements adding considerable strength. What this manual and the accompanying book are doing is to propose that we need to add an inspiring, bold and courageous vision that will help America pull out of this morass and overwhelm the developing negative and destructive forces, one that will REJUVENATE this country.

The Visions presented herein do not claim to be the be all and end all, and nor does it claim to be the sole wisdom. What these are trying to do is to begin a process of dialogue that will help unify all of the anti-Trump and anti-Republican movements, and inspire and motivate their participants and also new people who would like to help. However, it is intended to be a process that is ultimately good for all people – especially our native American, rural, women, working class, and communities of color. However, by also arguing that there needs to be a reform in how the rich and the powerful do things, they will ultimately be saved from their own destructive approaches and hence, hopefully, join the rest of the nation in unity.

This Book presents everything in much greater detail. If you are in a hurry, then download the Manual for free and get started. Then, if you need more information on a given topic, come back to this book.

SUMMARY - WHY WE NEED TO REJUVENATE & HOW

Rejuvenate means to restore and revitalize. After the hangover from Trump and Republican misrule lifts, America needs revitalize itself with a vision that is good for everyone, all of its lands and waters, and gets it to a place nationally and globally that is better for it and for the world. America desperately needs an alternative vision that learns from the strengths and problems of the past, realizes the developing dangers for America and the world, and develops a bold, courageous and vision that can inspire, motivate and get it to a place that is better for all of its people and for the rest of the world. All Americans need to think about where their nation has been, is today and where they would like it to go, so that the process is good for all Americans.

There is a vision out there that has emerged that is bent on demolishing everything that went before, that wants to damage or weaken all that many fought long and hard for – the democracy for all (including white Americans), the clean environment, the native American tribes, African Americans, women, and many others. Instead they want to redefine greatness and take America along a more fascist type path that seeks greater uniformity, removes all aspects that protect the environment, close its doors to immigrants, lets the financial robber barons steal all they can, and concentrate political and economic power in even fewer hands, and while using populist slogans to promise a false pipe dream of a better wealth and prosperity to all at the lower economic end of American society.

 The aim of this destructive vision is to do this even if this is bad for the rest of the world – supposedly America first. This vision is destructive for America itself and is bad for the rest of the world. By getting rid of financial regulations, the irresponsible financial behavior by robber barons will give us a worse version of the 2008 recession – a full-fledged Depression! Trump claims that his strategy on taxes, regulations, environmental pollution, and trade will create more better paying jobs – but this claim will be proven to be false – there be some short terms booms, but this strategy will fall flat on its face – its explained later below as to why! This manual and the related book present a better four-point approach that will create better paying jobs and be better for the economy – this approach will take the wind out of Trump's sails and hopefully convince many of his current supporters that there is a better approach. Encouraging white supremacy activities, arming everyone to the teeth with guns, polluting our environment, further militarizing the nation, and further enriching the rich will NOT lead to a better nation! While what went on before was not all satisfactory, and needs to be corrected, this destructive vision of his is taking the nation from the frying pan into the fire.

The aim of this manual and the accompanying book is to bring in focus all of the movements that oppose this destructive vision, to unite them, to alert them to the severity of the developing dangers, and to provide a vision and the ingredients that will be more than just a reaction and opposition to the above destructive vision. Whether they accept the vision laid out in this book or not, these movements desperately need a vision that is more than just opposition to Trump and the Republicans and gives them something that is inspiring and motivating to fight for. For more than a decade the Democratic Party has been losing elections and seats – the last election was not won by Republicans but it was lost by the Democrats – they need to really learn the lessons and revitalize the party! Perceiving the horror of what had happened, there have been many nation-wide marches and movements that were held, the latest of students nationwide reacting to the Parkland College shooting in Florida. The Democratic Party, including its newly energized Progressive wing, and these movements need to unite, develop a common strategy and pick up the flag of a common vision that they can all rally around. It is with this aim that this manual and the related book have been written. The manual is a summary and an action document, while the book provides a more detailed understanding of all the items, issues and strategies.

The United States of America has come a long way since it came together in 1776, gained Independence and formed a Union. The principles laid out in the Declaration of Independence and the Constitution were inspiring and provided the foundation for a nation that avoided all of extremes and evils of monarchy and religious persecution, while providing the beginning of a means of a people to rule themselves and change government and leaders peacefully. While all may not agree, there is little doubt that the principles and values established in the democracy produced a very vibrant and dynamic republic, that has grown to be the richest and most powerful nation on Earth – one that certainly dominated the world in the twentieth century.

However, there was much to complain about in the way that democracy was working in the US, and much that needed improvement. This democracy needs to be strengthened and the problems resolved, not gotten rid of as those with the destructive vision of America's future would like. Weakening democracy would be like throwing out the baby with the bathwater. So, understanding the problems with the democracy and the politics, and also for the losses of the democratic party over the last decade, need to be understood and remedied.

Further, it must be understood that rather than problems being resolved, the politics of the nation have gone from the frying pan into the fire. Very severe and dangerous trends have emerged with the coming of Trump that have fascist characteristics. These trends are characterized by threats to democracy, threats to diversity and a false rebirth, the language of violence, threats to freedom of speech, threats to women's rights (a masculine approach), threats to our economic future (increased corporate power), the rise of militarism and militancy, the related further proliferation of gun violence, and threats to our environment and our planet. Many of these trends are like what happened before World War II but in nations such as Italy and Germany. America escaped the extremes of fascism and communism by taking the middle path and undertaking to revitalize the nation through the strategies of a bold and courageous leader – Franklin Delano Roosevelt! At this point in the nation's history, these fascist trends need to be fought politically by all means possible, because they pose extreme threats to our democracy. But they can only eventually be overcome by a positive and constructive approach that takes the nation in a different direction!

A whole host of movements have sprung up in reaction to Trump and these horrific trends. Besides the Democratic Party (which needs to revitalize and reform itself and make itself more democratic!), there is the Progressive movement led by Bernie Sanders that showed great vitality in the last election. Then in addition, there are the activities of Resist, Indivisible, Move On, Labor and Union, Women's, African-American, Native American, Latin American, minority group, healthcare, environmental, hate monitoring and gun control movements. Each of these movements is active in its own way. All of them need to realize that they oppose the bad trends in the Republican party and the fascist trends that have come with Trump that succeeded in upending the Republican party through false promises, and aggressive and sometimes violent talk. The challenge now is for these movements to unite and develop a unified strategy.

But that is not enough. Beyond just reacting to Trump and the Republicans, we need a strategy that will set the nation on the path of genuine Rejuvenation, that will pull the nation out of the deep hole that Trump is getting the nation into and get it up and onto the path of a genuine revitalization that is good for ALL Americans and makes the nation beneficial for a world that has severe problems. If these movements have to not only consistently win elections, counteract the damaging and destructive vision developed by Trump, convince most of the electorate that they are better and have better ideas, AND then proceed to make America better through healthier politics, activities, and programs, they need a vision that will inspire, motivate and energize existing and new voters like never before. The attempt of this book is to get Americans started on the path of an alternative vision, that they can refine as they go along. The vision that is presented here takes what is already out there, strengthens it, and adds to it a strong strategy on jobs and economy. The alternative Vision that is detailed below a strengthening of democracy (stronger rights for ALL Americans, including whites), much better healthcare, strengthening respect for diversity, stronger women's rights, stronger minority rights (African Americans, Native Americans and all other minority groups), sensible immigration reform, a rejuvenation of the nation's environment, strong gun control and related violence, a climate change and environmental strategy that will Rejuvenate our land and the planet (this is more than sustainability and means making the land beautiful, clean, productive and supporting life), and a Defense strategy that meets the nation's security needs, helps world peace, that is more sensible and does not bankrupt the nation (right now, we are choosing "Guns over Butter").

How do we make it happen? Obviously, the main strategy is political. This manual needs to be in the hand of everyone: movements leaders, party leaders, candidates, elected officials, organization leaders, people politically active, and then last but not least, all voters and all citizens. This will provide an educational, unifying, inspiring and motivational tool in the hands of all active in seeking to overcome Trump and the Republican Party and seeking to take the nation on a better path. So, all of the strategies are needed and will be used: social media, website, traditional media (TV, Radio and print medias), organizational meetings of the movements, and political rallies. Every young person who is organizing (including the inspiring students demonstrating and organizing for gun control) should be armed with this manual. It is hoped that candidates for elected office, including those for president, use the arguments and rhetoric in this manual and use this vision to create their own related visions. Hopefully this manual and related book with energize, educate, motivate and arm political activists, citizens and voters to turn their country around, so that America provides a fair prosperity to all in a manner that is good for itself and for the world.

A Summary list of the Alternative Vision

- Better jobs and economy for all – but one that is pro-environment and pro-employment
- Protect financial system against robber barons - encourage only activity good for Main Street
- Cleaner America with national and global solutions for climate change
- A nation where all feel like first class Americans
- Common sense gun control is enforced and gun violence is made insignificant
- Women's rights are strengthened, with harassment discouraged and equality achieved
- A total reform of the criminal justice system - rehabilitation and decrease in prison population
- A Marshall plan for all depressed communities regardless of color
- Comprehensive immigration reform, with long term normalization of those already here, with some decrease in immigrant flows
- Support for revitalizing those nations from where immigrants are coming - better security and jobs
- American support for a rejuvenated world environment and economy, that benefits the poor and middle class the most
- Let a Stronger Constitution and Democracy Defeat Him Totally
    a. Fixing what we have – not letting him destroy it
- Strengthening A Major Pillar – The Fabric of Our Diversity
    a. Uniting to fight the disunity

- Truly Strengthening Our Defense & And Encouraging a Peaceful Cooperative World
    a. True strength together with our allies – building common cause with allies and world's nations – good for all
- Fighting for Climate and Our Environment
    a. Rejuvenating our National environment – air, water, soil and climate
    b. Rejuvenating and cleaning our planet – our only home
- Strengthening Women's and Social Rights
    a. Restoring gender equity and letting women decide
- Better Strategies for Jobs & Economy
    a. Four strategies that are better than Trump's
    b. Systematically create jobs, sustainably and with local community revival
- Strengthening Freedom of Speech & Press – the right to truth
    a. Defending an independent press and media to keep everyone honest and accountable to truth
    b. Educating the public about the issues, programs and trends
- Strengthening pensions and safety nets – Social Security
- Strengthening Healthcare – Medicare and Medicaid. Strengthening the Affordable Care Act and replacing with Universal Healthcare – the single payer capitalist system.

THE DANGERS POSED BY TRUMP & OVERCOMING THEM

Summary

America faces grave dangers to its well-being and maybe even to its nationhood! These are some of the dangerous trends that are emerging! With Trump as President, we face an incredible situation. While opposition builds, we need to understand what may be going on. After World War II, the word "Fascism" has generally been used in a negative way when describing opponents. Before the war, Fascism was born in Italy with the rise of Benito Mussolini and a version of it was adopted by Adolf Hitler in Germany, and we are all familiar with how that led to the second World War. During last year's US presidential election campaign, thoughtful writers like John McNeill had raised the question in Washington Post article (October 21, 2016) as to whether Trump was a Fascist. Based on his analysis, at that time he concluded that Trump scored high on the Fascism scale, scoring 26 out of a possible 44 points. So, how fascist is Trump and is he heading the nation towards fascism? To answer that, we take a detailed look at Fascism and at the evidence.

How does one recognize Fascism? Wikipedia described one of the definitions of Fascism as follows: "One common definition of the term focusses on three concepts: the fascist negations of anti-liberalism, anti-communism, and anti-conservatism: nationalist authoritarian goals of creating a regulated economic structure to transform social relations within a modern, self-determined culture: and a political aesthetic of romantic symbolism, mass mobilization, a positive view of violence, and promotion of masculinity, youth and charismatic leadership." Fascism is basically a system of government that believes that liberal democracy is obsolete and wishes to replace it with something more totalitarian, is authoritarian, and emphasizes a rebirth back to a prosperous and secure golden age that has racist undertones.

Before we begin it is fair to say that we should be listening to the financially strapped and struggling small business Americans in rural and small-town USA, and farmers that were devastated by George Bush's financial crisis of 2007-2008, and were not helped by the recovery that happened under Obama, and who voted for Trump. It is important that we reach out to them and as we organize, find ways to meet their socio-economic concerns in ways other than what Trump appears to be outlining. We have to begin to bridge some of the divide in this highly polarized nation, as we proceed to tackle the negative challenges thrown up by Trump. At the same time, the Democratic party needs to reorganize and reorient itself in order to meet the needs of a big percentage of this population. There is no reason why the rural areas should be red.

We take a look at the evidence in terms of the threats to democracy, the threats to diversity and minority rights, the use of the language of violence against opponents, the patriarchal approach that is basically anti-women, the disinformation campaign of using and spreading "alternative facts", intimidation of the press, an economic strategy that consists of bullying and promising big business more and that makes promises of more jobs by wrong approaches, an attack on the social security net in terms of social security and healthcare, and a militaristic approach that may create more problems globally than it would solve. The use of rebirth rhetoric of "Make America Great Again" has focused on better jobs and encouraging business. But it also has racist undertones, that is also trying to get us back to the 1950s with an anti-environmental and anti-climate change approach that will devastate not only the US, but also our Earth. In each case we look at the fascist aspect and what we need to get organized to do.

Threats to Democracy

Besides the US Constitution, all important legs of our democratic system of government have come under attack – the judiciary, the

legislature and the press. Besides that, the presidency has been cheapened and debased. Fascist movements discard liberal democracy, or any form of democracy.

One of the biggest strengths of the US has been the Constitution, the democratic system and the rule of law. By most definitions, besides opposing other forms of government, Fascism opposes democracy and tries to get rid of it at the earliest opportunity. Right from the start of the Republican Primaries Trump began to attack democracy by claiming that the primaries were "rigged" and that he would not accept the results of the voting if he lost (the very basis of democracy). There was not a word from him about that after he won the primaries. Then during the main election campaign, he continued to claim that the elections were "rigged" and that he would not accept the results of the election if he lost. The US presidential system of government is really that of a republic, where the Electoral College and not the popular vote determines the winner. Anyway, after he won the election in the Electoral College, but lost by about 2.8 million votes in the popular vote, he continues to argue that nearly 3.5 million votes were cast illegally and fraudulently, although all of the election commissions of all of the states have stated that nothing of the sort occurred.

Actually, what he is doing is an extreme version of what the Republican party has been trying to do for many years now, or voter suppression - that is to suppress as many of the eligible voters from voting in the categories that are unfavorable to them. Combine that with gerrymandering of legislative districts (drawing the legislative map of districts that ensures that Republican candidates win), and democracy is weakened. **The threat to democracy is very real as Trump is trying to undermine the very confidence in the whole democratic system – not just the politicians in Washington.** Court decisions, first that of a judge of Mexican national origin and then those relating to the travel ban, were attacked – so we need to ensure that the checks and balances imposed by our Judiciary and the rule of law prevail! Even the

Republicans should beware! What we really need is a reform of the system on the lines that Bernie Sanders has outlined, like reducing the influence of big money, and possibly a replacement of the Electoral College by a system based on the popular vote. What we do not need is the weakening of our democracy – on this we must fight Trump tooth and nail.

Then as Bernie Sanders has done, we need to get the influence of money out our national politics, fund elections through public means, give equal time access to all candidates, otherwise we will have the dissatisfaction of the democratic process that we have today – the control our democracy by the rich and powerful through the backdoor. Election and democratic reforms are very essential at this stage, and we should be emphasizing and fighting for these at the same time as we are trying to rally round the pillars of the constitution and democracy. We must not allow Trump to weaken our democracy that encourages and unleashes the energies of most of our population.

Threats to Diversity & A False Rebirth

Time and again, history has shown us that nations have done well that have welcomed many different points of view and have empowered all minorities and made them feel like first class citizens. Trump has attacked the nation's pillar of strength based on diversity. Besides this, he harps about a return to a previous golden age – "Making America Great Again" – this has always been a hallmark of fascist movements.

When the masses immigrated from Europe, many were escaping from religious persecution and bigotry, and different forms of slavery. That is why, after the American Revolution, when they wrote the Constitution, there was a strong emphasis on religious freedom – the freedom of everyone to practice their own religion in their own way without threat of persecution or domination. Also center stage was the emphasis on Freedom – free speech, freedom to assemble and freedom to associate. Since then the nation has accommodated, although after struggles, the rights of women, and the rights of blacks. Then, after World War II, over the last 70 years the nation has welcomed immigrants from all over the world, until the nation has begun to almost reflect the world. Most of this immigration has been carefully regulated and legal. The respect for diversity is America's greatest strength - it makes all welcome, to follow the "American Dream" of prosperity through hard work, and to contribute in some way to America. The US does need a new immigration policy that leads to orderly immigration, of a type and size that is in its best interest – but not one that weakens the strength through diversity.

Now this respect for diversity is under attack. The lost age syndrome, or the taking of the nation back to some period of past greatness has been a hallmark of all Fascist movements. In the case of Hitler, it was some return back to an age of Aryan superiority, and the cleansing needed to restore that purity and its assumed greatness. Trump's let's "Make America Great Again" is a rebirth call that supposedly aims to take the US back to an age when it was great and white, and because of that, prosperous and globally dominating. There is little wonder that white supremacist groups like the KKK (Ku Klux Klan) have responded with glee! This has further emboldened the KKK to increase its hate filled anti-minority talk and actions. At the same time, instead of trying to come up with a sensible immigration policy that would solve the problem of undocumented immigrants, would meet the needs of the current population, while meeting the future needs of the nation, he has pandered to racial hatred against Hispanics in general and people of Mexican origin in particular.

Next, he has used the fight against terror, mainly now coming from the Islamic State group but also from other Islamic groups like Al Qaeda, to spread hatred against Muslims. In so doing he is also taking an irrational approach to refugees from nations that have severe conflicts, like Syria. Rather than focusing on combatting the terrorist groups, and coming up with ways to wean people away from radicalization with ideological approaches that aim to convince them of better ways, he has tarnished all Muslims, and has been portraying this as some sort of religious war. The danger here is that he will scapegoat and victimize minorities, especially Hispanic and Muslim, and create a sense of fear in the country, leading to internal turmoil and instability – this may actually make the country less safe, as minorities withhold information from Homeland Security officials about possible terrorist attacks. Since his election campaign began, hate crimes against all minorities have greatly increased as some of his supporters have been encouraged by his talk.

With the induction of people with a white supremacist background to his inner circle, there is cause for alarm, as all the diverse groups from all of the world may face the brunt of discrimination and persecution, and the civil rights of African Americans and other minorities may suffer. Although the Muslims and Hispanics may be the first is line, it appears that all non-white and non-Christian groups may be next. The rest of the world looks up to America because of its respect for diversity and because it welcomes people from all the regions of the world with open arms. We have to fight to restore respect for diversity and the protection of immigrant and minority groups.

The Language of Violence

Trump used the either vulgar offensive language or the language of violence against his Republican opponents, and then against Hillary Clinton during the presidential campaign. This sort of intimidation of opponents is again typical of fascist tendencies. Although this has not always been the case, in democracies, violence within nations and the use of violence on other nations has generally been used as a measure of last resort, when all else fails. On the other hand, the approach of Fascism is to encourage the use of violence in politics within the nation, and externally by war, portraying a supposed masculinity. Trump implicitly encouraged violence against his political opponent when he said that the second amendment folks would take care of Hillary Clinton (the second amendment to the US Constitution is the right to keep and bear arms or weapons). Further down in the campaign he initiated calls to "lock her up", and if elected, promised to prosecute her on the issue of emails. The use of the language of violence is unacceptable in a civilized democracy, and is an approach which must be criticized and discouraged in every way. The real danger is the possibility of the use of violence against minority groups, immigrants, "Black Lives Matter" types of movements and political opponents – any movement in that direction needs to be watched like a hawk, and effective counter strategies developed at every step.

Threats to Freedom of Speech and Press & Alternative Facts

In a free and democratic society, the press and media have the duty to hold the leaders accountable, and make sure that the truth is exposed. Instead, Trump has been attacking the press all the time. He and his Alt-right supporters have the biggest generators of conspiracy theories and fake news, and then have criticized the media for exposing them. They practice the strategy that if a lie is told often enough, it will be believed – a strategy followed by Joseph Goebbels, Hitler's propaganda chief. For sure, the media needs to freed from the clutches of Corporate domination, but that does not mean it should then fall into the clutches of the Government and political leaders, to be solely used as their propaganda mouth pieces!

Trump has consistently attacked the media at every stage, especially when it has highlighted or brought attention to information that was not in his favor. He has consistently used the words, "Crooked Media" to criticize the media. Instead at every stage, Trump has published statements which now his supporters are calling "Alternative Facts". The most recent incident was that of the small crowd size at his inauguration, versus that of Obama, and the much larger crowd size at the Women's March the day after his inauguration. In spite of all evidence, photographic and otherwise, to the contrary, Trump and his supporters continued to claim that the crowd size at his inauguration was much bigger than published by the media. Joseph Goebbels, Hitler's propaganda minister practiced the art that if one told a lie often enough and forcefully enough, that eventually it would be believed. The propaganda campaign of the Nazis was designed to have their population believe whatever they put out to the public. It appears that they have adopted this approach. Early in the campaign Trump claimed that Muslims in New Jersey had openly celebrated when the 911 attacks took place in New York. From all evidence available to public and otherwise shows that this did not happen. Fake news like this has become quite common. Pizzagate was a totally debunked conspiracy theory saying that emails revealed by WikiLeaks that linked a number of restaurants and members of the Democratic party to a child sex ring – a person who actually believed it had shown up with a gun at one of the pizza restaurants, only to find to his surprise that nothing of the sort was going on.

Besides the dangers of spreading "Alternative Facts" and "Fake News", there is a real danger that the administration will attempt to suppress and intimidate the press, in order to always have its version of the story get out to the public. The biggest danger is the distortion of intelligence to throw out untruths or half-truths that are then used as an excuse to go to war, as happened before the Iraq war in regard to weapons of mass destruction. The intimidation of the press is growing – just recently Trump's senior advisor Steve Bannon, asked the media to shut up and listen. We have to be ready to fight for the freedom of the press and the freedom of speech, otherwise one of the strengths of our democracy will have been weakened, and false information and fake news will become the norm.

Threats to Women's Rights & The Macho Approach

In this nation's history, women fought hard before they even got to vote. Women have fought hard for some rights which are the right to their body and life (Choice), the right to privacy, the right to bodily integrity, and the right to determine when and how to reproduce. All of these rights are under attack. This represents a masculine approach that has been typical of fascist movements.

Millions of women marked nationwide and around the world in the Women's March that was held the day after Trump's inauguration. This was to protest the growing alarm at the erosion of women's rights that women had long fought for and many aspects of his political agenda. One of the hallmarks of Fascism is its patriarchal approach to society, where women's issues are viewed through the viewing glasses of masculine men. Women have fought hard for some rights which are the right to life, the right to privacy, the right to bodily integrity, and the right to determine when and how to reproduce. In the early days of the Trump administration, executive orders were issued that curtailed the use of funds internationally for abortion. Further expected are the de-funding of Planned Parenthood, which provides a range of medical services generally to all women, but especially to pregnant women, and a change in the healthcare laws so that insurance plans will not support healthcare for reproductive services. All of the pro-choice gains made in recent years are being reversed, so that women will have much less latitude in decisions that affect their bodies and their health. Again, there is a need for dialogue with pro-life folks that are anti-abortion to see if there can be some middle ground. Maybe pro-life should expand to include the life of the mother, kids dying in poverty, and the lives of animals.

Threats to Our Economic Future

Fascism aims at a regulated economic structure, based on self-reliance through protectionist policies. All of Trump's policies point in this direction, through trade interventions and proposed tax cuts. The large financial institutions and corporations are being favored – they will pocket the money and know how to make greater profits with fewer people. The reductions of regulations mean a repeat of behavior by large financial companies of the risky behavior that gives them higher profits, but results in another major financial crisis, like the one in 2008. Trade and tax policies need to become pro-employment and pro-environment, and not be anti-employment and anti-environment, and pro-big multi-national business interests, as they have been! We have to fashion strategies to help our rural areas, and our depressed communities and those who have suffered income and asset losses over the past decade, to free them from the clutches of his fascist trends.

Trump mainly won the election in battle ground states because of his promise of higher paying jobs with a revived industrial type economy. While the big tax cuts and infrastructure spending will increase growth and jobs in the short term, there are many dangers lurking. The first is the high probability that with reduced regulations and lax enforcement, large financial institutions will again engage in irresponsible behavior leading to another financial crisis like the one we had in 2007-2008 under the Republican administration of George Bush. This led to the biggest recession since the great depression, and in spite of government efforts under the Obama administration, these financial reforms are still not in place to protect us from another crisis. The second danger is that with his massive tax cuts, the US federal deficit will grow much faster, as revenue from increased economic activity will not make up for the revenue lost by tax cuts.

After World War II, the US economy was such that because of its economic and industrial superiority, and an industrial infrastructure largely intact, developed an economy and industrial system that not only created wealth for the rich, but also a large and growing mass of people who entered the middle class that enjoyed a good standard of living, and not least because they became the consumers of the output of the system. There are two reasons why this era of relatively high paying jobs and affluence for a big middle class slowly came to an end. The first was that at every step even as the US and the global economy grew, companies learned through automation and productivity changes, to grow and make higher profits with fewer and fewer workers. The second trend was that as the global trading system grew, companies of the richer developed nations not only got the poorer developing nations to open their markets so they could sell more to them or in them (which was what most trade agreements led to), but they were also able to move their manufacturing operations overseas to lower labor and environmental cost areas, thus reducing well paid employment in their home countries, but also making them more competitive relative to their global competition.

What Trump is claiming that he can good jobs back to the US by getting the companies to move their manufacturing operations back to the US. While this may work in the short term (although it will increase the production costs of companies, and prices US consumers pay), the problem is the bigger trend that has led to job decreases has been that the companies have learned through automation and other means to do the same tasks with fewer people. These jobs will never come back unless the whole financial system is overhauled to encourage employment. That's why Trump's efforts to encourage companies to grow and relocate manufacturing plants back to the US, will never work in generating enough high paying employment – as the same companies will turn around, pocket the increased income and profits and do it with even fewer people!

What part of his approach is beneficial and what needs to be fought? His approach for increasing higher paid manufacturing jobs or those that give higher wages is certainly a crying need for America. Trade agreements need to be re-negotiated so as to have a stronger component of labor and environmental rights, and not just those favoring the large companies in the richer countries like ours at the expense of much of their populations. America needs to favor a re-industrialization that takes makes tax laws and approaches that make American companies more competitive, encourage exports, makes increased employment profitable more profitable than increased automation, and emphasizes more local production (agricultural, industrial and processing) for local use. Unless the tax, government and industrial policy favor higher manufacturing employment, Trump will not be successful in creating enough high paying jobs to fulfil his promises during the election campaign. The regulatory and government based financial burdens for small business should be decreased in a thoughtful way, while taking reasonable steps to make sure that environmental and safety concerns are met. This should not be like Trump's approach of doing away with most regulations without serious thought and analysis. Also, the big influence on big money and lobbyists on politics, that Bernie Sanders has railed against, will not diminish unless he moves in the direction of election and democratic reform – that is the best way to drain the swamp.

This is where the Democratic party is very weak and has nothing in its rhetoric that supports any of this. They have to have a strategy that thinks and favors how the economic and financial machine of the country and world work, goes to favor good behavior that improves economic conditions without destroying the environment and discourages irresponsible, speculative and bad behavior, like that which led to the financial crisis. Corporations need a strong code of ethics that emphasizes their duty to strengthen democratic rights while protecting the health, safety and economic well-being of their employees, and the cleanliness and health of the environment. Then, as Bernie Sanders has emphasized, we need to proceed the full course on financial reforms, break up the large financial institutions, so that if they engage in risky behavior, we let them fail and that does not endanger the US and global financial system. The Democratic party needs to add a strong approach that favors the type of industrialization and re-growth that it favors. This will take the wind out of Trump's sails. Unless it does so, and includes Bernie Sander's progressive change items, it will not make a comeback.

Till now, Trump's approach is to bully everyone in sight: The company in Indiana shipping jobs overseas, high cost defense contractors, and nations like Mexico by attempting them to simply pay for the wall he plans to build while slapping unilateral tariffs or taxes on goods coming from Mexico. Government information from the US Trade Representative indicates that "Mexico is currently our 3rd largest goods trading partner with $531 billion in total (two way) goods trade during 2015. Goods exports totaled $236 billion; goods imports totaled $295 billion. The U.S. goods trade deficit with Mexico was $58 billion in 2015." The right way is to renegotiate NAFTA (North American Free Trade Agreement) with better environmental and labor rights clauses, or one that may bring more jobs back to the US. Trump has withdrawn from the TPP (Trans Pacific Partnership) that included 12 nations – this was intended to open each other's markets in a number of areas, while strengthening things in a number of areas. The main objectives were not only financial but also, by excluding China, it was to reduce economically and then otherwise China's strategic influence – what Trump appeared to want. By withdrawing from TPP, he has made things more advantageous for China – the opposite of what he said he would do. We should reach out, re-negotiate some clauses in the TPP to add some labor rights, call it something else, and still go through with it.

By his bullying approach and his threat to impose unilateral tariffs or import taxes (which are illegal as per existing agreements), he will set off trade wars as other nations retaliate with similar measures. This type of protectionism is one of the factors what led to the great depression of the 1920s. The fascist aspects that may emerge here is that he appears to be proposing an economy where he sets the rules, rather than pass laws and encourage and regulate industry according to those laws.

The social danger from the viewpoint of opponents, is a reversal of all of the social and safety net gains that they have fought for, for many years – Women and LGBT rights, Social Security, Medicare, Medicaid, and Affordable Health Care – this will see many of his supporters suffer also as they will see their self-funded pensions and safety nets weaken, while not seeing enough of good paying jobs. The economy does best when both the supply side (making sure business can supply the goods) and demand side (making sure that people have money to buy) receive attention. The reason why the US economy does better under Democrat administrations is that they pay attention to the demand side, but do not neglect the supply side (business is encouraged but with environmental and labor safeguards). The reason why the US economy does not do as well under Republican administrations is that they attention to the supply side, but severely neglect the demand side – people do not have money to buy, so the economy suffers. This becomes obvious if one looks at past US data. Instead, Republican administrations embolden business to engage in irresponsible and risky behavior to make big profits, leading to financial crises.

The Rise of Militarism & Militancy

There is little doubt that the US has the most powerful and capable military in the world, and the only one that has global reach – it also spends more than the next seven nations put together. However, Trump has begun the misuse of the US military, threatening its use at the slightest provocation, and passed a big increase in the defense budget. This again is typical of the strong-arm militarist approach that is typical of fascist governments. He is also politicizing the military which can have a

demoralizing effect on its morale. Further, by alienating our allies (which represent a significant part of our strength), he is weakening US defense.

Fascism has always had a very strong militaristic approach, both within nations and externally. While a nation should be strong enough to meet its external security challenges and those of its allies (who also represent the nation's external strength), its approach should always consider the need for cooperation with its allies. Trump's statements appear to indicate a militaristic and strong man approach. He favors quick military action against ISIS, without understanding the complexities of engaging in conflict in yet another country. He has appointed members to his cabinet and advisors in the security and defense area generals who are known for their expertise and reputation as good combat commanders.

US Military strength comes from the fact that it has the most powerful and most capable armed forces in the world. According to Wikipedia, as of 2011, the US Defense budget was about $ 700 billion, out of which about $ 541 billion was the base budget and the rest was budget for contingency wars overseas. Wikipedia stated in 2016 that, "The Department of Defense spending in 2010 was 4.8% of GDP and accounted for approximately 45% of budgeted global military spending – more than the next 17 largest militaries combined." The other main factors that add to the US military strength are its massive superiority in terms of weapons technologies in all areas of technology over its competitors, its military alliances and security agreements with many countries in the world (mainly NATO countries, Australia, New Zealand, Israel, South-east Asian nations, and many other nations around the world), the fact that it is the only nation that has armed forces commands in all areas of the world (seven regional commands), and the general perception around the world that its tries to be an honest broker (most of the time) in areas of conflict around the world. The main area that the US needs to pay special attention to is the possession of nuclear weapons and delivery systems that could devastate the US, especially from Russia, and the proliferation of nuclear weapons and materials to other nations and groups.

It is false to say that the US military has weakened under the Obama administration. Its posture may have been less in terms of engaging in armed conflict abroad than that of the George Bush Administration, but the annual US Defense budget continued grow under Obama. ISIS, that is mainly active in Iraq and Syria militarily, is only a terrorist threat elsewhere, and does not constitute and existential threat to the US (does not threaten its existence). However, Trump used the example of ISIS and blew its threat way out of proportion in order to create the illusion that the armed strength of the US had diminished. ISIS and other Islamic groups need to be fought on the ideological, moral, and socio-economic fronts – not just on the middle-east battle fields and on internal security fronts. Trump is weakening the US military strength by making statements that weaken our alliances with other nations, principally the NATO countries. Other allies are worried by his statements which may weaken our alliances – this represents a real weakening of US strength.

Regardless of how one feels about this, the US has been the custodian of world peace since the second World War. However, it also true to say that currently, the US is a nation at war – in Afghanistan, in Iraq, in Syria and in smaller ways around the world. Nations around the world look to the US to address security concerns in their neighborhood because it has always appeared to be an honest broker. It is false to say in this regard that the US has not been aware of and taken its own interests into account. However, Trump's America first policy and the recent travel bans from seven Muslim majority countries is weakening its position globally as the custodian of world peace, and is making the world a much less safe place.

For the second World War, the world was fortunate that a sleeping giant like the United States of America was out there to fight against Nazi Germany and its allies. In the current situation, there is no nation in the world (with the exception of Russia in the nuclear weapons area) that can stand up to the United States. So, if the US wants to engage in military actions of an oppressive or dominating nature, militarily at least it would face little opposition. Hence, the responsibility increases for citizens of the US to stand up and oppose any military actions that Trump may take globally.

Many will argue that the US defense budget is too big, and that it should be trimmed and US should stop dominating other parts of the world. However, for this, the US needs to establish and maintain new global security arrangements with all of its allies and other nations. With Trump, we are headed in the other direction, where even the security arrangements that have mostly maintained peace since World War II are being weakened, as our allies watch in consternation and alarm. Further increases in the Defense budget will only lead to what is called Imperial Overreach, where a great power ultimately goes into decline by spending too much on defense and gets stretched too thin compared to the threats it faces, which under Trump may increase.

Threats to Environment and to Our Planet

The US had made massive progress in cleaning up its environment for the smoke stack days, when its air and water were severely polluted and all the toxic waste locations polluted around the country being designated as Superfund Sites. The nation had also made much progress in beginning to reduce greenhouse gases like carbon dioxide. Now Trump is doing everything he can to reverse this progress - this means a more polluted environment in the US, and a lack of leadership by the US internationally. His approach to Climate Change can be called "The Great Leap Backwards"!

We have to realize that we live on Planet Earth with 195 other nations. Since World War II, we have been the leaders of a system of global governance and influence that has worked well for the world, and kept the peace – especially in our favor. Rather than become totally selfish and only looking out for ourselves, we can actually do well and strengthen affairs around the world if help and work with many of the poorer nations around the world to solve global problems – in this way, we will not have a growth in the refugees from many of these nations as their nations and economies fall apart.

By giving the green signal to both the Keystone XL pipeline and the Dakota Access pipeline, Trump has indicated that fossil fuels are now back in the game and will be used to supply the world with energy, jobs and profits. While this may provide jobs and profits in the short term, this will be a big blow to the efforts to slow global warming. The same is true of his efforts to revive coal, which is an even greater contributor to greenhouse gases for every unit of energy it provides.

Global warming is not some distant or possible future problem. It has already begun to devastate the US and the world. The increased temperatures lead to increased evaporation and more energy in the atmosphere – this increases the force and rain related to natural disasters like hurricanes, tornadoes, and coastal storm. The hurricanes are getting stronger and more devastating like hurricane Katrina ($ 75 billion losses), and Superstorm Sandy ($75 billion losses). In regard to tornadoes, it has been noted that the number of tornadoes in each super cell (cluster) of tornadoes has been increasing, making them more devastating – this happened in the southeast US early in 2017. Out of 59 sites recording rainfall, six sites set all-time records (National Oceanic and Atmospheric Administration – NOAA data). In recent years, many rainfall events in the Chicago area have led to very high levels of rainfall – some to flash flooding. In 2016 many parts of the world – India, China, Russia and others experienced record heat waves, and the temperatures have been rising year after year. Global warming is not some distant problem – its devastation has already arrived and is going to get worse, unless we begin to solve the problem. The solutions are all there – clean energy (renewable energy – solar and wind - increased energy efficiency and some properly managed bio-fuels) and a lower carbon economy. We cannot solve it by moving in the other direction.

The US signed on to the Climate Change Treaty that was first established in Rio de Janeiro, Brazil in 1992. Besides talks and agreements and protocols (agreements to act), there was little progress in solving this problem till December 2015, when nations signed the Agreement in Paris. More than 180 nations around the world, after much delay and effort, finally came together to begin to solve the problem of global warming. We have to fight Trump to make sure that he does not gut this effort in order to try and achieve economic rejuvenation of the US – but to pressure and steer the world towards clean energy, clean jobs and clean growth! Clean Energy (solar and wind energy, and energy efficiency) has done so and can create many more jobs than reviving coal. **The planet and mother nature do not lie, and anyone who continues to deny the threat of man-made climate change will be proven wrong by nature.** We only have one planet Earth that supports our life and that of all living things – we cannot let it be trashed, for in so doing we trash ourselves. Jobs versus environment is a false argument we can have both, as long as our progress is of a sustainable type. On this score, he must change course, or we must fight Trump at every stage.

Why the threat of Fascism Will Remain after Trump

The fascist trends described above are a real concern – damaging US democracy, achieving advantage by engaging in political verbal violence, encouraging militarism, weakening women's and minority rights, intimidating the press, and pandering to the racist tendencies among groups that will create social turmoil and instability in the US. On the socio-economic front, common folks will suffer from a weakening of healthcare, Social Security,

Medicare and Medicaid – leading to greater poverty and privation. On the financial front, there is the combined danger of another financial crisis and trade wars that could lead to another global depression. The tax "reform" will lead to tax cuts, not create good paying jobs, massively increase the federal deficit. On the environmental front the biggest danger is the worsening of global warming, as the baby steps that the world has begun to take with the Paris Agreement of 2015 begin to unravel and other nations increase their carbon emissions. On the international front, the militarism will lead to bad adventures that will make matters worse and weaken us militarily.

Trump has encouraged the wrong kind of political movement that will continue to plague this nation long after Trump leaves or is removed from power. Many of the groups affiliated with him and supporting him politically are now energized. Our challenge is to make sure this does not reach the kind of situation that led to the second world war, with the USA replacing Germany as the World's trouble maker!

Beginning the Fight to Overcome

Trump's win has created an ecstatic response among his supporters, and hope among those who had lost out economically for many decades, and especially in a big way after the Bush caused financial crisis of 2007-2008 that had caused the worst recession since the great depression. The Republicans are ecstatic that they control all three centers of power – the Presidency, the Senate and the Congress, and get to appoint Supreme Court judges of their liking and those that agree with their social agendas. While this has shaken up the Presidency, and Trump promises many unconventional approaches to all aspects of political life, there are many dangers that have surfaced.

The rule of law itself is being threatened, first by rump interfering and intimidating the FBI and the Department of Justice in investigations in which he may be involved. About a hundred former intelligence and FBI officials have criticized his action to revoke the security clearance of John Brennan, former head of the CIA, and have criticized the politicization of the Rule of Law. Next, about 350 newspapers throughout the country have published editorials criticizing Trump's attacks on the Press and on his attack on the Freedom of Speech!

Out of all the problems discussed above, we can see that the biggest danger of all is the Fascist tendencies that he is showing – damaging US democracy, achieving advantage by engaging in political verbal violence, encouraging militarism, weakening women's and minority rights, intimidating the press, and pandering to the racist tendencies among groups that will create social turmoil and instability in the US. On the military front, the biggest danger that the nation and the world faces is that of Trump in control of the most powerful machine in the world. Before, Hitler and Mussolini were defeated by America and its allies. Now, America itself could become that danger to the world under the banner of fascism. On the socio-economic front, the biggest dangers are reduction in health care support by repeal of the Affordable Care Act, and a weakening of Social Security, Medicare and Medicaid – leading to greater poverty and privation. On the financial front, there is the combined danger of another financial crisis and trade wars that could lead to another global depression. On the environmental front the biggest danger is the worsening of global warming, as the baby steps that the world has begun to take with the Paris Agreement of 2015 begin to unravel and other nations push ahead like Trump's stated policy for the US – increase their carbon emissions, and let the global environment be damned.

What has made America great to date has been religious freedom, respect for diversity, its economic strength, its military strength, its offering of economic opportunity, and its ability to be a leader and honest broker in world affairs. While it has not always upheld these strengths, and there has sometimes been some abuse, it has mainly held the course, and built up an international order that has maintained the strength of America and its allies. To be sure, there are many US and global problems still needing to be solved in the security, political, social, financial, trading, environment and development areas – and there is much that can be done to make it fairer, more environmentally sustainable, beneficial for all, and lead to a system of international security arrangements that would ensure a just and lasting peace.

But we need to pull together to fight the Fascist tendencies that are emerging. There has to be an active resistance to his agenda by fighting to protect health care, opposing his regressive cabinet appointments, protecting immigrant rights, protecting the environment and our Earth, providing clear education on issues, demanding justice and civil rights, demanding that government departments provide us with correct and accurate information, and fighting to protect the press from attacks. We have to make sure that we succeed in emphasizing that diversity of every kind is our strength, and that respect for religious, racial and cultural diversity makes us a better nation.

Next, we have to watch Trump's Fascist tendencies like hawks and fight them at every stage whenever we see his proceeding in that direction. A really worrisome aspect is the encouraging of violence, by hinting at it – we have to come up with effective strategies of counteracting it if his supporters engage in violence. One of the biggest directions that we need is freedom of speech – the First Amendment to the US Constitution. First amendment rights of every kind must be protected and fought against at every stage. Freedom of the press must be fought for at every stage, even while we reduce the strong domination of much of our press and media by corporate interests – and especially strengthen public broadcasting that does not financially depend on advertising. Second Amendment rights advocates should be made to understand that nobody is taking away their guns – just that there needs to be common sense gun reform. Then as Bernie Sanders has done, we need to get the influence of money out our national politics, fund elections through public means, give equal time access to all candidates, otherwise we will have the dissatisfaction of the democratic process that we have today – the control our democracy by the rich and powerful through the backdoor. Election and democratic reforms are very essential at this stage, and we should be emphasizing and fighting for these at the same time as we are trying to rally round the pillars of the constitution and democracy. We must not allow Trump to weaken our democracy that encourages and unleashes the energies of most of our population. It's a time to come together and organize to make all this happen.

THE LESSONS OF THE PAST – BEFORE TRUMP

The United States of America has come a long way since it came together in 1776, gained Independence and formed a Union. The principles laid out in the Declaration of Independence and the Constitution were inspiring and provided the foundation for a nation that avoided all of extremes and evils of monarchy and religious persecution, while providing the beginning of a means of a people to rule themselves and change government and leaders peacefully. While all may not agree, there is little doubt that the principles and values established in the democracy produced a very vibrant and dynamic republic, that has grown to be the richest and most powerful nation on Earth – one that certainly dominated the world in the twentieth century.

However, there was much to complain about in the way that democracy was working in the US, and much that needed improvement. This democracy needs to be strengthened and the problems resolved, not gotten rid of as those with the destructive vision of America's future would like. Weakening democracy would be like throwing out the baby with the bathwater. So, understanding the problems with the democracy and the politics, and also for the losses of the democratic party over the last decade, need to be understood and remedied.

Here in summary are the pillars of nationhood and the problems that had developed, and the trends that have worsened things for a majority of Americans and what political trends caused Trump to come to power. For each issue, the items needing attention are listed, and then these are detailed below in the visions section.

The US Constitution & Its Amendments

The US Constitution was established on September 17, 1787, and it consisted of a total of 7 Articles. Since then it has been amended 27 times to take care of different issues, or establish a Bill of rights to protect citizens, make sure that women, blacks and youth could vote. Initially only white propertied males could vote. This was expanded so that all whites could vote. Then blacks and women had to fight often in the streets in order to win the right to vote. Nonetheless, the checks and balances of the different parts of government, the Presidency, the legislators and the judiciary were designed to act as a check on each other. The legislatures were to establish the laws, the President was to enforce and implement those laws while acting as commander in chief, and the judiciary was to interpret the law, and ensure that the rule of law prevailed.

Significant Problems & Issues

While the US Constitution is one of the strongest written constitution documents in the world and has served the USA well, it must be said that every right had to be fought for in the streets. Even Slavery was eliminated by the Thirteenth Amendment to the Constitution, it was not until the 1960s that African Americans got the right to vote with the passing of the Civil Rights Act. The Native American Tribes of America, who have suffered much, sometimes total extermination since the coming of the immigration from Europe, have been at the receiving end for all of history, and treaties with them have been consistently violated. IF the condition of some parts of the population are bad, the conditions of Native Americans on and off the reservations are just terrible. Before the Citizen's United ruling by the Supreme court, politics had become dominated by money through lobbyists, but after the ruling, this trend grew astronomically by allowing insane amounts of money to influence democracy – allowing the US democracy to become a government "Of the rich, for the rich and by the rich". **Items Needing Attention:** The US Constitution should be protected, and as necessary, strengthened by additional amendments. The US democracy should be strengthened by all means possible, so that in Lincoln's words, the Government is truly, "Of the People, for the people and by the people". That is the way to true power to the people – Trump's way is that of populism (claiming to do things for the underdog) while trying to impose a dictatorship. The influence of money on politics has become insane and needs to be kicked out of politics – it's a misinterpretation of the First Amendment that money is allowed to be allowed first amendment rights – how about the first amendment rights of the poor? See visions below.

Historical Global Misuse of Power

Although much happened before World War II, after the war, there have been many situations when the USA has intervened, supposedly in its own interest, politically and militarily to interfere in the internal matters of other nations. To be fair, although some may disagree, the nation has mainly done a lot of good in the world, from the Marshall Plan for Europe, to helping with the Ebola epidemic, establishing NATO and containing communism, helping the Asian tigers prosper, and sometimes coming down on the side of democracy. The list of foreign interventions is a long one, from the CIA sponsored assassination of the democratically elected leader of Iran and installing the dictatorship of the Shah of Iran, to the overthrow of governments and the support for despotic dictators, Philippine president Marcos, Chilean President Pinochet, Panamanian President Noriega, etc. The misguided Vietnam War was a clear example of conducting a war while misinforming the American public – in that case, it took the anti-war riots and the eventual defeat in Vietnam that ended that war. The misguided war in Iraq was built on a great deal of misinformation by the Bush Administration, that created more problems than it solved, and many claim that it led to the rise of ISIS (Islamic State) – we are still living with the mess today! The practice of using drones to assassinate Islamic terrorists with bombs, together with the collateral damage, is not something that the UN approved – but his practice continues today, with the American people not knowing what is really going on. This is the first time that the US has been at the receiving end, with Russia interfering in our election, and if we want Democracy and the power of the people to prevail, we have to fight this interference tooth and nail. **Items Needing Attention:** It is very important that we, the American people, that, unless the mainland America is under attack, DO NOT allow a president or the armed forces to start any war, without the permission of congress and also a referendum voted on by the people. Trump must not be allowed to start a war on Iran or a war in Korea – everything that he claims must require proof, as very little of what he says can be believed. We cannot send our soldiers in harms way to satisfy the desires of the extreme right of the Republican party, with us and the world left to clean up their mess. The practice of using drones in foreign nations should require a process of international and national approval. Missile attacks, like occurred on Syria after a recent charge of their use of chemical weapons, should require international and congressional approval. These issues are discussed in visions below.

Problems with Republican Party Politics

The Republican party of today is no longer the party of the days of Lincoln. It is no longer sensitive to the problems and issues of poor people (white or non-white), minorities and native Americans. After fighting against the rights of blacks to vote, they have tried every means possible to suppress the votes of minorities. They have gerrymandered the voting districts, or drawn the borders of districts in such a way as to ensure that they have a majority in congress. Reagan's economic strategies led to the rise of homelessness for the first time in America – in fact he may be called the father of homelessness.

Before the mid 1990s, in spite of their differences, at least the politicians of both parties talked to each other respectfully and politely, while agreeing to disagree (which is the way democracy is supposed to work. Then, starting in the mid 1990s Newt Gingrich started the trend of viciously attacking people of the other party, including the president. Since then, with the exception of people like John McCain, the Republican Party essentially continued the trend of vicious personal attacks on opponents. Then, with the coming of Trump, in the name of doing away with political correctness, Trump has used vicious, abusive and at times violence filled language to attack even his Republican opponents.

They claim to be for "Free Trade", which means the ability of big companies to be able to sell and produce where they want, so that environment and employment suffer (Trump's talk aside, his emphasis in both Tax cuts and trade is to help the big guys earn more profits). They falsely claim to be the party that creates jobs, and one that is better for economy and business. Global military strength and domination, and starting unnecessary wars are a big part of Republican emphasis, so military spending grows by leaps and bounds, military contractors earn more and more, even if it busts the budget. In this case, and for creating bigger and bigger prisons, Republicans want big government. Republicans are big supporters of the NRA and receive massive election funding from them – which is the reason they are captive to the NRA and unable or unwilling to reduce the gun violence plaguing this nation.

When it comes to healthcare, protecting ordinary people from companies engaging in predatory practices, or meeting the minimum needs of poor people for income and housing, the Republicans want small Government, and claim to be fiscally responsible (That means balancing budgets), except that with large increases in Military spending and big tax cuts, they end up creating bigger federal deficits. While it is true that the spending of public funds should have accountability, transparency, and an absence of corruption, spending less on these is a primary cause of why the US economy does much worse in Republican administrations. You see, Republicans push supply side economics, which means that they neglect the financial needs of most of population, so most of them have little or no money to spend, so sales and business suffer. Also, the relaxation of regulations during George Bush's time, meant that the robber barons stole what they could get their hands on while the government looked the other way. This lead to the deep recession of 2008 – it's the Republicans that caused it and caused the massive pains suffered by the middle class and the poor – which is what helped Trump to win – and now Trump is going to make it worse by doing this even more and giving the robber barons a big tax cut, which will not generate adequate jobs.

Problems with Democratic Party Politics

This is not the place to discuss the issues that the mainstream Democratic Party stands for, these are discussed below as part of the Vision for America. However, the Democratic Party has also been quite heavily dominated by Corporations and financial interests. This was especially true during the Bill Clinton years in the !990s. Also, it ignored the needs of African Americans by passing legislation that lead to an explosion of the prison population with Latinos and blacks. Corporate interests again dominated when Obama failed to move aggressively against the financial companies that had engaged in immoral, and sometimes criminal behavior, and failing to punish them enough. The leaders of these companies essentially were not punished for their criminal acts, and instead the middle class the poor paid the price for the recession of 2008. To the credit of Obama and the Democratic party, the US did recover much faster from the big recession, and went from 800,000 job losses a month to slow but steady job growth throughout his eight years. Job growth has continued at about the same pace during Trump's rule, but the basis had already been set during Obama's administration. Obama could have done much more if the Republicans had not been so obstructionist, creating the grid lock that Washington has become famous for – the Republicans are responsible for gridlock. Both from the viewpoint of decency and honesty, the Democratic Party was a lot better than their Republican counterparts.

However, the Democratic Party went into a big downslide even in the Obama years. They lost more than a thousand legislative seats country-wide and ended up only dominating the governorships and legislatures in about 6-7 states. **The election is 2016 was not so much won by the Republicans as it was lost by the Democrats.** The reasons for the big losses were (this is based on an autopsy of the democratic losses in 2016 by the progressive wing of the party): That the party chased after Republican voters and neglected its main base, working class families, people of color and the youth; it lost the support of African-American women; its support among young voters was affected by GOP voter suppression, depressed economic conditions and poor messaging on how these conditions were going to be alleviated; its **undemocratic policies and use of superdelegates in the presidential election turned off most of the progressive voters;** its refusal to directly challenge corporate power and deal with corporate misbehavior sternly; and its hawkish stance in supporting Republican military mis-adventures turned off many working class families that had suffered.

The Democratic Party is not gaining much enthusiasm among its base, by being timid in confronting Trump – the Republicans opposed Obama much more on everything, and for eight years their sole purpose was to obstruct Obama, and so they even did not agree to things they would normally support. The Republican party claims to be the party that knows how to create business growth and jobs. **While being strong in supporting safety nets (healthcare, social security and Medicare), the Democratic party is very weak in the area of Jobs and economy, which is why it lost many working-class voters who felt abandoned by the party. The party needs the strong addition of a message on Jobs and Economy – how to directly create jobs in manufacturing, depressed communities, and sustainability activities, that contrast well with the Republican approach – see vision below.**

Overall Problems with Politics in General

The US political process has generally served the nation well for more than 200 years. However, there is a need to improve it significantly. Some of this is outlined in Visions below. From an overall viewpoint, the entire democratic process needs to be more participatory. Candidates promise one thing in elections and do something different when in office. Constituents should have some means for keeping them accountable between elections, like having significant issues and votes in congress being subject to open consultation with constituents before voting. **The main disease that is afflicting US politics is the big influence of big money, that has been made easier by the Citizens United Supreme Court Decision.** There is a desperate need to get rid of the influence of money in elections, the influence of money through lobbying (Citizens United needs to be reversed, and laws passed to limit the direct and indirect paths to political funding), limits on billionaires being able to buy elections (limits on how much of their own money they can use), the influence and control of the media, and laws that level the playing field for candidates (such as equal time on TV and radio, besides debates). Next, the undemocratic process of electing the president through the Electoral College needs to be gotten rid of, and everything should be based on the popular vote. There needs to be a strong emphasis that bad, abusive and violent language will be strongly discouraged in elections, and candidates and politicians who engage in it will be strongly reprimanded and discouraged from this behavior. There needs to be a strengthening of election laws for this. Lastly, as Eisenhower had warned us, the influence of the military-industrial complex in society needs to be strongly reduced and separated from support for troops and first responders. The insane growth in the military budget under Trump has to be reversed – even many defense experts think that it is bad for the nation, as it creates great risk in terms of the exploding federal deficit.

An Economic System that Concentrates Wealth & Impoverishes Many

Overall, the entire economic system in the US and the world, is designed to concentrate wealth with the rich! The investment rules, the trade rules, the power provided to the companies, all concentrate income and assets and political power in the hands of the big companies, and big financial institutions. **The problems of** the US come not from immigrants taking the jobs of others, but that the companies make bigger and bigger profits with fewer and fewer people, and sacrifice the income, health and safety of the vast masses of people – the working classes, the employees and labor. They then engage in risky behavior that causes financial crises! To solve these huge problems, economic, social and political power must be more equally shared and financial and other companies must behave and be subject to rules that ensure that their behavior is only for the public good.

THE MOVEMENTS & THE CHALLENGE OF UNITING THEM

In Opposition to Trump, there has been an upsurge of marches and movements that have spawned, many that were not there before. The first was the massive Women's March in Washington DC and around the country. The turnout in the capital was more than that at Trump's inauguration! Since then there have been many marches, including the Climate March and the recent march against gun violence. The challenge now is to unite these movements and turn them into a positive, effective and constructive political force that will overcome not only Trump, but the Republican party and their billionaire funders and Super PACs. These movements should know that they have to unite and work together to overcome, and turn the marches into something truly historic, wiping out and reversing the wins by the Republican party, and winning the electoral battles so as to take back the Congress, the Senate, the majority of the states, and eventually the presidency. If they come together, these movements will be able to have a higher level of success. The Democratic Party is in a lead role, but it needs to expand its tent and accept all of these movements into its fold, or to develop a clear cooperation with them in both election strategy and platforms.

The objective here is to present a summary description of these movements and describe some common threads, along with a link for each.

Resist
In their own words, "Resist is a foundation that supports people's movements for justice and liberation". They started with the opposition to the Vietnam War and have now expanded to supporting all such movements. Resist has become a symbol of resistance to Trump.
https://resist.org/about/mission

Indivisible

Indivisible started in response to Trump winning the election and the realization that all of the progressive aspects of national life and politics were under attack with Trump and the with the Republican controlled Congress and Senate. They learned from how the Tea Party organized within the Republican party and helped stall the agenda of Obama and the Democrats. Their big contribution has been the Indivisible Guide that has given people who want to be politically active a guide on how to apply pressure on their Members of Congress (MOC). This guide has been used to focus and apply grassroots anger against the legislative agenda of Trump and the Republicans. Their efforts and guide has had a significant impact on fighting that, but they have not generated enough pressure on the Democratic members of Congress to stand up to Trump in every way. Indivisible is also a very effective rallying call to the American people to unite and not allow themselves to be divided. Here's the link to the guide:
https://www.indivisible.org/guide/

Our Revolution

This is the movement related to Bernie Sanders' bid for presidency. In the words of the website, their Mission is: "Our Revolution will reclaim democracy for the working people of our country by harnessing the transformative energy of the "political revolution." Through supporting a new generation of progressive leaders, empowering millions to fight for progressive change and elevating the political consciousness, Our Revolution will transform American politics to make our political and economic systems once again responsive to the needs of working families. Our Revolution has three intertwined goals: to revitalize American democracy, empower progressive leaders and elevate the political consciousness." Their website contains the best and most comprehensive descriptions of positions on most issues. These provide excellent descriptions of progressive solutions to the nation's issues.

https://ourrevolution.com/about/

Progressive Democrats of America (PDA)

PDA is affiliated with Our Revolution. It is active nationwide to get truly progressive candidates elected, each of whom is evaluated by responses to questions before a particular candidate is endorsed. They oppose democrat candidates who may be too beholden to corporations or financial interests. Some of the issues that they are fighting for are universal healthcare, passage of the Equal Rights Amendment (ERA) for women's rights, stopping global warming, voter access and election integrity, and ending wars and occupations.

https://pdamerica.org/our-issues/

Black Lives Matter (BLM)

The Black Lives Matter movement started in response to the killing of young black men by police and is focusing on racial profiling, police brutality, and racial inequality of the criminal justice system. It appears that whenever people talk about being tough on crime, they usually end up being tough on young black people (mainly young black men). Perceived insensitivity to reform of the criminal justice system of the Hillary Clinton campaign may have cost her a significant proportion of the black vote, and voter turnout among blacks was much lower than for Obama. In their words, the BLM global network is a "chapter-based, member-led organization whose mission is to build local power and to intervene in violence inflicted on Black communities by the state and vigilantes." Its structure is very decentralized. It is characterized as a new civil rights movement, that appears to speak for other minorities too, and that distinguishes itself from the older traditional black leadership characterized by church involvement, democratic party loyalty and respectability politics (Wikipedia). In that sense, it actually is a movement that is behaving as if all lives matter but drawing attention to the particularly atrocious conditions that black people face in the criminal justice system.

https://blacklivesmatter.com/about/

Color of Change

The Color of Change is a non-profit civil rights advocacy group that was formed after Hurricane Katrina, to give a stronger voice to African-Americans in politics. It describes itself as the largest online racial justice organization. In its mission it emphasizes that its aim is to create a more favorable atmosphere for black people by influencing leaders in companies and in government. It works in the areas of encouraging and fighting for more economic and media justice, and a fairer and just response in the criminal justice system. Color of Change has fought for the restoration of voting rights that impact black people the most, and especially the voting rights of those formerly convicted but have served their time or are on probation.

https://colorofchange.org/about/

Women's Rights Movement

The day after Trump's inauguration, the nationwide Women's March highlighted not only women's issues but also national issues. In Washington DC, the turnout was larger than at Trump's inauguration. Historically, by the 1820s and the 1830s, the right to vote had been extended from only propertied males to all white males regardless of how much money or property they had. After that, women have had to fight every step of the way for greater equality. After almost a century of protest, women finally won the right to vote by the passing of the 19th Amendment to the US Constitution in August 1920. That November nearly 8 million women voted for the first time. The next fight is for ratification of the Equal Rights Amendment to the US Constitution, which would grant women tights equal to men in matters of divorce, property, employment and other issues. Only one more state has to ratify the ERA and it becomes law.

But Women's rights issues on the Democratic Party side are much wider than that. The National Organization for Women (NOW) supports reproductive rights and justice (abortion rights, access to contraception, economic justice, ending harassment and violence against women, racial justice and LGBTQ rights. Reproductive rights mean that women should have the right to choose what happens to their bodies in the reproductive process - access to abortion, contraception, family planning services, and reproductive education. The harassment of women has gained a new prominence, and in case after case, whether in companies, media or government men who harassed women have to exit or resign. But somehow Trump manages to survive even though he is reported to have harassed many more women than them. The challenge is to convert the anger shown in the Women's marches into a strong political showing in elections and in issues.

Move ON

Move ON is a progressive public advocacy group and political action committee founded in 1998. As per Wikipedia, MoveON.org Civic Action provides education and advocacy on national issues, while MOveON.org Political Action is a political action committee that contributes to the campaigns of candidates. In 2014 they tried to get Elizabeth Warren to run, then supported the candidacy of Bernie Sanders, and after that it launched a "United Against Hate" campaign in an attempt to stop Trump from being elected. Move ON has been very active with protests, rallies, and political advocacy on the progressive side, and organizes petitions. Move ON organizes as groups of councils, and has over 250 councils nationwide, and at least one in every state.
Civic Action: https://front.moveon.org/about-moveon-civic-action/
Political Action: https://front.moveon.org/about-moveon-political-action/

Gun Control Movement

Gun rights versus gun control have a long history for the nation. The Second Amendment to the US Constitution, the Right to Bear Arms states that , "A well-regulated Militia, being necessary to the security of a free State, the right of the people to keep and bear Arms, shall not be infringed." In the early days, each state had a militia and the national army had not yet gotten established, and the amendment was intended to enable each of the states to maintain a militia and for each of the militia members to continue to possess arms. However, the gun rights advocates maintain that this is a right of individuals to possess arms that cannot be controlled by the state and argue that military style assault weapons (that can kill many people quickly) are included in this right. They claim that the right to engage in sporting activities (hunting, practice shooting, etc.), the right to protect themselves from criminals, and the right to protect themselves from the tyranny of the state. The National Rifle Association (NRA) has been a powerful political force in lobbying and influencing the issue and has fought back many attempts to even small sensible efforts to control guns, and their resulting violence.

Gun violence has reached epidemic proportions in the United States. No other developed nation has the level of gun ownership or of gun violence as the US. Efforts to have the Centers for Disease Control (CDC) monitor gun violence, injuries and deaths as a public health issue have failed, so that adequate data is often not available on this issue. There have been many efforts to control guns, and many efforts to expand gun rights over the years. The legislations have gone back and forth on these sides.

The main issues that gun control advocates are fighting for are the expansion and tightening of background checks, the inability of criminals, mental health sufferers, terrorist list people, etc. to buy guns, the banning of assault weapons, reduction of concealed carry laws, the expansion of mental health care, and greater responsibility of gun owners to keep their guns form being misused by others. If gun rights folks want to engage in sporting activity and to protect themselves, then one hand gun and one shot gun, both properly registered and controlled, should do it – why any more than that?

Florida's Parkland School massacre of students has ignited a massive gun control movement, much of which is being spear headed by students. In a short time, they got some response in terms of the banning of bump stocks, getting many businesses to break connections with the NRA, and some tighter gun laws in Florida. This movement represents a real opportunity for the gun control side to gain some advantage, but the gun control movement needs to unite with the other movements described in this section if they are to be effective in elections and in changing the laws and their enforcement. Here is a list of some of the main movements:

1. Everytown for Gun Safety
2. Moms Demand Action for Gun Sense in America (started after 2012 Sandy Hook shooting)
3. The Brady Campaign
4. Americans for Responsible Solutions
5. Law Center to Prevent Gun Violence
6. Coalition to Stop Gun Violence
7. Never Again (started after Parkland College, Florida deaths)

The main challenge this time is to take the new momentum of the above gun control activists, motivated anew by the Parkland students, and show it as political strength.

The Native American Movement

The Native Americans are the original inhabitants of America. Geological history indicates that they migrated over the ice bridge formed between Asia and North America during the last ice age, some 10,000-20,000 years ago. Anyway, they lived and developed as tribes in North America for thousands of years before the coming of European settlers. During their time the land was an environmental paradise, with dense forests, wetlands and prairie. American Indians have been one of the most mistreated groups in America, from outright annihilation, forced evictions, relocations, treaty violations, and after that mistreatment, impoverishment, and insecurity.

The American Indian Movement (AIM), was formed in 1968 to address treaty, sovereignty, and leadership issues while fighting against racism and police harassment of Indians when they moved away from reservations. AIM also focused on the preservation of American Indian culture and their economic independence (Ref.: Wikipedia).

The Immigration Movements

Movements have come up to support the rights of immigrants and aim at Immigration reform. Earlier from about 2006 onwards there have been massive immigration type marches, but hey have so far not been able to move the Republican controlled Senate and Congress to solve the immigration issues in a manner that is good for the nation. As per Wikipedia, the Fair Immigration Reform Movement (FIRM) is a coalition of 30 immigrant rights movements aiming at comprehensive immigration reform and protecting the civil rights of immigrants. It also struggles for improvements in the lives of marginalized communities of race, color, gender and ethnicity. MoveOn.org and three other lead organizations partnered with more than 150 organizations in organizing the "Families Belong Together March" on June 30, 2018, that had massive marches occurring at about 750 locations throughout the US.

Climate Action Movement

Few issues can break the back of our civilization than Climate Change. Al Gore's Climate Reality organization was one of the early ones, as Al Gore attempted to keep the issue alive through talks and movies such as "The Inconvenient Truth". Then came 350.org the main force behind which was Bill McKibben, which organized rallies around the world. Climate Action Lobby aims at influencing legislation to make it more climate friendly. The Peoples Climate Movement organized the Peoples Climate March in 2017 in about

200 cities in 2017, to protest the policies of the first 100 days of the Trump presidency.
https://peoplesclimate.org

Other Movements
Union movement and Working Families Party -
http://workingfamilies.org/about-us/
Democracy movements – Center for Popular Democracy -
https://populardemocracy.org/our-work/issues/all
POCLAD – Program on Corporations Law and Democracy -
http://www.poclad.org
SPLC – Southern Poverty Law Center – Monitoring and exposing
Hate groups - https://www.splcenter.org
Occupy Wall Street
ACLU – American Civil Liberties Union - https://www.aclu.org
People's Action - https://peoplesaction.org – a coalition of many grassroots progressive orgs
Opposition movements that need to be countered– Republican party, Tea Party, Breitbart, KKK, NRA, and Koch Brothers

REJUVENATING AMERICA - DETAILING THE VISION

Making America Better by Strengthening Democracy, Diversity, Economy, Environment, Women's Rights & Defense

Our nation faces historical challenges that will determine whether our future is good politically, socially, financially, environmentally, and militarily – with, peace, prosperity, idealism and security, or whether we do into sudden or steady decline – the end of the American era. It will also determine whether the increasing inequality of income can be reversed and whether those at lower end of the income and asset scale will get the minimum needed for their basic needs and for enjoying sustainable livelihoods. What we do now is therefore super important.

So, what this book is doing is starting the process of building an alternative vision of a better America – We start with a Bold, Constructive & Positive Approach on which we can build upon!

Summary

The abuses against democracy and the attacks on the rights of Americans require the strengthening of our Bill of Rights and enhancing the power and well-being of all of the people of America. Besides direct actions and opposition along the lines of RESIST and Indivisible, the best approach to defeating Trump is to go in the other direction, and positively strengthen everything that has provided greater democracy, strength, peace, and economic growth – reinforcing it with a strong emphasis on Jobs and Economy (methodically, in a fair, innovative and sustainable way - that also increases the wealth and assets of those at the bottom of the economic ladder) aimed at weaning away those Trump supporters who voted for him on this basis, while cooperating economically with most of the rest of the world. Namely, to Rejuvenate America!

Rather than giving power back to the people, Trump is leading like a dictator, by weakening democracy. There are significant efforts to strengthen democracy - these are the fight for voter rights, eliminating gerrymandering, and complete campaign finance reform. These must be strengthened in every way and go beyond just counteracting his efforts and those of the Republicans. To these we must add the issues of adequate healthcare for all; significant and effective gun control accompanied by social and health actions, actions on climate change, clean energy and environment; strengthening Women's rights; strengthening the diversity that is the bedrock of our democracy; strengthening minority rights, strengthening the rights of Native Americans; strengthening the well-being of all; fair, sensible and humane immigration reform; a jobs and economy strategy and industrial policy that is genuinely pro-employment, pro-environment , pro-sustainability, and pro-small business; strong ways of directly reviving depressed communities; and a Defense Strategy that maintains US strength, cooperates with our allies, without excessive spending and promotes global well-being and peace through cooperation and a shared prosperity. This will be a powerful way of bringing all of the movements together, motivating them, helping them make common cause, and cooperating to build a United States of America that is good, not only for itself and ALL of its people, but as a shining light for the rest of the world.

Why the core values need to be strengthened

- The core values of democracy of the people, secularism, bill of rights, human rights, and genuine freedom need to be added to.

- We need to proceed further to make our Democracy truly of, for and by the people – ALL of these aspects need to be strengthened. We need to remove past weaknesses!
- We need to strengthen religious freedom, and the absence of the misuse of religion by the state – this also means strengthening secularism – respect for religions of all.
- We need to strengthen Diversity in every way – ALL citizens should feel like first class citizens, regardless of race, religion, national or ethnic origin, gender, and sexual orientation. Even non-citizens should be guaranteed some minimum basic rights
- We need to establish the firm foundation and strategy that ensures that all have the opportunity and resources to meet their own Basic Needs - healthcare, education, legal rights, and security.
- We need to have a strategy for Jobs and Economy that is truly pro-employment, pro-small business, pro-environment, revitalizes our depressed communities, and creates jobs by rejuvenating, and transforms all human activities to solve climate change problem and rejuvenate all our global ecosystems – land, sea, and air. This needs to in a full way address changing tax reform, trade strategy, investments, R&D, and commercialization in order to provide all who want and need it the opportunity for interesting work and an adequate livelihood.
- We need to take care of our own people much better and not let the big financial interests and companies continue to dominate and take all of the wealth. Investing in the education, skills and health of all of our people must be a high priority. Only investments on Wall street that help Main Street should be encouraged. Financial and corporate activity needs to be within strict rules of the game that ensure that risky, irresponsible financial behavior is regulated and punished – nationally and globally.
- We should again resume our leadership of the world, but this time, we should lead the world to better place

environmentally, financially, security wise and socially. We need to be the leaders and the cooperators that make good things happen globally. At the same time, the world order should discourage and penalize misbehavior – with strong international institutions that are capable of doing this.

Strengthening Our Democracy

Republicans continue to falsely raise the bogie of big government and criticize Democrats as big tax and spenders. The truth is that Republicans favor big government when it suits them (big military spending – supporting a War economy, even when there is no war – or else go create a war that ends up creating a bigger mess), and imprisoning more and more people (directly attacking the well-being of minorities). At the same time they try and reduce the safety net by continuously attacking and trying to reduce what benefits the vast majority of the people – Social Security, Medicare and Medicaid. They also want to reduce protections for common consumer people, from the financial companies that try to behave in a predatory fashion. It has taken a long time through the Clean Water and the Clean Air Acts to make this nation's environment clean and healthy – it had become very polluted – acid rain, smog, superfund toxic waste sites, ground level ozone, etc.). So, Trump has trashed all the regulations that protect the people from pollution. Social Security, Medicare and Medicaid are NOT entitlements – they are a form of government protected pensions for folks that work all their lives, and Medicare and Medicaid need to be replaced by Universal Healthcare.

We need a government that is FOR ALL the people of the nation. We need a government that is big enough to police the financial sector and the big companies to make sure that they follow the rules, the rules are such that they prevent the robber barons among the big actors from stealing money by risky and predatory behavior, provide a basic minimum in terms of a safety net, and make sure that the infrastructure is not only well maintained but transformed into the low carbon economy of the future. We need a government that is large enough to make sure the rule of law is enforced, but the destructive prison system needs to be reformed and the emphasis needs to shift to rehabilitation, especially for small time non-violent offenders. And yes, we need smaller government when it comes to a reduced military budget, as described in the section on defense.

All of the current efforts of Trump and the Republicans aimed at voter suppression, gerrymandering, buying elections and financially dominating our democracy have to be soundly defeated. Then we have to support and strengthen all efforts that strengthen Voter Rights, end Gerrymandering, and Reform Campaign Finance Reform (Defeat and reverse the ruling on Citizen's United). Voting rights should be strengthened by encouraging, enabling and empowering people to register and vote. Tom Steyer's' efforts to motivate and register the youth to vote and efforts by all progressive organizations along these lines should receive a high priority. We should begin to push two amendments to the constitution. The first is the Right to Vote, so that no citizen can be denied the right to vote. The second amendment would make it illegal for for-profit corporations to make political contributions and enable congress to create public campaign finance system. Then, the electoral college system of selecting presidents should be abolished and presidents should be elected on the basis of the popular vote.

We in America have for long strutted about that our democratic system was the best. However, the truth is that some of its flaws have become obvious. On a fundamental basis, in order to improve the quality of our democracy, we need to pay attention to its breadth, its depth and its range. The proportion of the people that participate in the decision-making processes determines the breadth of the democracy. The depth of the democracy is determined by the quality and fullness of their participation. And the range of democracy is determined by what matters of community life can be influenced by participating members and he extent of their influence and authority in these matters. We should evaluate the quality of our democracy and see how we can improve it. This requires a more fundamental look at this than can be done to justice here.

Let a Stronger Constitution & Democracy Defeat Him – Totally

All of the current efforts of Trump and the Republicans aimed at voter suppression, gerrymandering, buying elections and financially dominating our democracy have to be soundly defeated. Then we have to support and strengthen all efforts that strengthen Voter Rights, end Gerrymandering, and Reform Campaign Finance Reform (Defeat and reverse the ruling on Citizen's United)

Strengthening Voting rights

https://en.wikipedia.org/wiki/Voter_suppression_in_the_United_States
Voter suppression is rampant in the US. It is the attempt by Republicans to discourage or keep citizens from registering to vote, or making it difficult for them to vote. In state after state, Republicans have tried every means, in the name of preventing voter fraud, from getting those groups to vote that oppose them. The false claim is that there is voter fraud – in case after case, it has been shown that there is little if any voter fraud. Donald Trump's Presidential Advisory Commission on Election Integrity, formed in May 2017, supposedly aimed at voter fraud, is really another attempt at voter suppression. His claim of 3.5 million fraudulent votes cast for Hillary Clinton in the 2106 election was falsified by all the state's election commissions – yet he continues to spread these lies. If the votes cast for Clinton were fraudulent, could not the votes cast for him in the states that he won, be fraudulent? His claims of voter fraud, also cast doubts on his own legitimacy. He is

taking voter suppression to a new height. This is another of his attacks on the democratic system.

It therefore becomes important, not only to fight all these attempts at voter suppression but to go further in encouraging and empowering and enabling ALL citizens to vote. Although it may be tough to achieve, it may be good, for strategy purposes to push for the Right to Vote as an amendment to the Constitution (which it is not), and in the articles relating to that, lay out in clear terms what protections are to be accorded to citizens so that their votes cannot be suppressed. All legal and legislative schemes that aim at voter suppression (in the name of voter fraud), must be defeated.

Not only have all barriers to voting by all have to be removed, we have to proceed towards measures that would facilitate, encourage, help and motivate ALL citizens to register, vote, and educate voters on their rights. We need to think through things from the ground up and see what actions, plans and programs would encourage almost all of the people to participate in the political process and make their participation meaningful and effective, not only in elections but between elections. To improve the quality of our democracy, we need to pay attention to its breadth, its depth and its range. The proportion of the people that participate in the decision making processes determines the breadth of the democracy. The depth of the democracy is determined by the quality and fullness of their participation. And the range of democracy is determined by what matters of community life can be influenced by participating members and he extent of their influence and authority in these matters. We should evaluate the quality of our democracy and see how we can improve it. This requires a more fundamental look at this than can be done to justice here.
See the link on voting rights
https://advancementproject.org/issues/voting-rights

Eliminating Gerrymandering

In 33 out of 50 states, the state election commissions are dominated by partisan party affiliations. The parties in power there have used computer software to create gerrymandered districts that would ensure that they would win in those districts – districts, whose geographic boundaries were selected in very detailed ways (never in straight lines) to include within the district, only citizens expected by election statistics and other available knowledge to favor their own party. The two techniques have been described as "packing" and "cracking" – packing is where the opposition voters are packed into one voting district, so they could only enable one opposition legislator to be elected – cracking is where the opposition voters are spread across many voting districts, so that their votes would not matter.

We must now take every measure to reduce or eliminate gerrymandering in the USA. We have to have neutral redistricting criteria that are not influenced by politicians. Redistricting plans must not violate the Equal Protection Clause or the Voting Rights Act of 1965. Someone has proposed the use of Metric geometry to measure gerrymandering. A Missouri citizen has proposed that the US Census department that shows equal population and the most compact geometry for each district. This eliminates gerrymandering and is based on the GPS coordinates of the population (Ref.: Wikipedia – Oct., 2017). The state election commissions have to be taken out of political hands, and put in the hands of non-partisan election commissions.

In state after state, we have to fight gerrymandering and make sure its adverse effect on our democracy is eliminated.

Ending the Buying of Our Elections

Unwise rulings and self-serving decisions have led to situation, where our elections and our democracy are almost totally dominated by big money of rich billionaires, and large financial interests. **It has become a democracy of the rich, for the rich and by the rich!** We need total and comprehensive Campaign Finance Reform. We have to end the buying of our elections by big money – we need to end the influence of money on politics and especially on political campaigns. We know that the Bipartisan Campaign Reform Act (BCRA) of 2002 (McCain-Feingold) was struck down by the Supreme Court on constitutional grounds in the Citizens United vs Federal Election Commission ruling (March 2009). We have to not only support all efforts to complete Campaign Finance Reform, but have to proceed in the other direction with other ideas.

Here are some **alternative ideas** that were listed in Wikipedia that are worthy of consideration like voting dollars, matching funds, clean elections, and a constitutional amendment that would outlaw the use of for-profit corporate money.

1. **Voting with dollars**
   The voting with dollars plan would establish a system of modified public financing coupled with an anonymous campaign contribution process.

2. **Matching funds**
   Another method allows the candidates to raise funds from private donors, but provides matching funds for the first chunk of donations. For instance, the government might "match" the first $250 of every donation. This would effectively make small donations more valuable to a campaign, potentially leading them to put more effort into pursuing such donations, which are believed to have less of a corrupting effect than larger gifts and enhance the power of less-wealthy individuals. Such a system is currently in place in the U.S. presidential primaries.

3. **Clean elections**

Another method, which supporters call clean money, clean elections, gives each candidate who chooses to participate a certain, set amount of money. In order to qualify for this money, the candidates must collect a specified number of signatures and small (usually $5) contributions. The candidates are not allowed to accept outside donations or to use their own personal money if they receive this public funding.

4. **A Constitutional Amendment**

   This proposed amendment would outlaw the use of for-profit corporation money in U.S. election campaigns and give Congress and states the authority to create a public campaign finance system. Unions and non-profit organizations would still be able to contribute to campaigns

Other ideas are to eliminate the Electoral College system for US presidential elections. This system is archaic and needs to be abolished. True democracy demands that the US president be elected on the basis of the popular vote.

Superior Strategies on Jobs & Economy

Overcoming his rhetoric with a 4-point strategy that will succeed!!

Why Trump's strategy will fail

Trump's strategy for jobs and economy will fail for a number of reasons: (1) Tax cuts for companies or any jobs brought back from abroad – the companies will pocket the money – they have learned how to handle larger profits and do it with fewer people, and (2) Lower regulations means that many big financial companies will steal large sums of money by creative financing, leading to a financial crisis bigger than that in 2008 – leading to bigger job losses than 2008.

Why the Economy Does Better Under Democrats

The US economy does much better under democrats (past history during democrat and republican presidents is proof), because of a number of reasons. Republicans follow supply side economics where they try and make things financially favorable to businesses and the rich, who supposedly provide the supply of commercial goods and services. However, the problem is that they neglect the demand side and insist on the rest of the population doing with less, so the people do not have much money to spend, and there is a limit to how many consumer goods the rich buy – this is actually bad for business and leads to recessions.

Under democrats, the economy does better because while not neglecting business, they follow demand side economics where the major strategies are putting money in the hands of the vast majority of the population. The people have money to spend and they spend most of it as they need the basic and consumer goods, so consumer demand is much stronger and businesses benefit

Overall Background – How We Got the Job Losses

Without getting into much controversy, at this point, the best thing may be to describe what strategies have been employed, politically and financially till now and then describe the alternatives. With regulations loosened under the junior Bush administration, and existing regulations being not properly enforced, the financially powerful corporations engaged in risky behavior that reaped immense profits for them, but nearly led to a collapse of not only the US but the global financial system. **This was the biggest short term destroyer of jobs – as many as 800,000 jobs were being destroyed per month when Obama took over as president. If Trump had taken over as a president then, we would have been in a full scale Depression! President Obama was faulted**

for not coming down harder on the people who engaged in financial misbehavior – Trump would have been even more lax!

Both the actions of the Federal Reserve Bank in terms of adding liquid funds to the economy, infrastructural investments done by the Obama administration, and direct actions by the administration, such as bailing out the US Auto industry (thanks to the Obama administration), helped turn things around, from what nearly was a full scale depression – all caused by financial institutions when they were being poorly policed. President Obama's actions helped turned the economy around from a major recession to a recovery with very significant job growth. The hangover from these big excesses of irresponsibly reducing regulations on financial businesses and not policing them enough, are still with us and with the coming of the Trump administration, this same process can repeat, and the danger of this happening has surfaced again.

Imagine a baseball game with few rules and referees that don't enforce the rules – what would you have – chaos! That's what we got from Bush – now with Trump it's even worse! Capitalism works well when the rules of the game are strong and well enforced. The danger of a recession or even a full-scale Depression for the US and the World is the biggest danger facing the world economic system today! **It not only needs tough regulations of financial businesses, a decrease in their sizes (so that any one business going bankrupt due to misbehavior does not affect the big economy), and tough enforcement of regulations – not just in the US, but globally, as misbehavior in any part of the world hurts everybody – especially people at the bottom of the economic and financial ladder!** This is what the masses revolting globally against globalization should be fighting against the most – little regulation and poor enforcement of financial rules.

Besides such catastrophic actions, the pillars of the economic strategy and conventional wisdom has been that of providing tax depreciation for capital equipment investments, and especially those that reduce the labor content. The argument always has been that of increasing "productivity" as measured by the output per unit of labor. So the argument goes, if the "productivity" is increasing, the economy must be doing better. Productivity has seldom been measured as increases in output per unit input of capital or as output per unit input of energy – if these are looked at, these are usually as an afterthought. But increases in labor productivity inherently mean less labor content and hence fewer jobs. This is a sure recipe for job losses – in fact, this has been encouraging job losses.

https://www.forbes.com/sites/washingtonbytes/2017/03/28/how-the-government-perversely-encourages-physical-over-human-capital/2/#58c114d83360

From 1980 to 2014, US manufacturing lost about 7 million jobs – most of it to this approach.

The other strategy that has been pursued is that of immense infrastructural spending that provides short term jobs in construction, but might occasionally also help improve the efficiency of the economy. Usually this spending by government creates jobs in the short term, and may have some effect of pump priming the economy, to get it moving again. But usually, infrastructural spending only gives short term job gains while the government is spending money. Also, most of this infrastructural spending will be on roads that favor the automotive mode of transportation, which is known to be a big contributor to carbon emissions and worsening climate change. We need more infrastructural spending on other lower carbon transportation modes.

After World War II, the capitalist economies established GATT in 1948, the General Agreement on Tariffs and Trade. Both

GATT and the deal that established the World Trade Organization (WTO) in 1995, were processes that were dominated by big governments and big business. Small organizations, and non-profit, environmental and non-governmental organizations had very little influence. As a result, environmental, labor and employment concerns were disadvantaged, and suffered. For example, the US had very strict standards on the levels of herbicides and pesticide residues allowed on agricultural imports – but WTO watered these down and reduced these levels in a big way, so as to favor international agri-business. Also, the poorer heavily indebted developing countries, who often were under the domination of the IMF (international Monetary Fund) and the World Bank, were usually at the receiving end and usually had to open up their economies in exchange for very little from the rich developed nations.

The same things happened when the US established trade agreements with other nations or established NAFTA, the North American Free Trade Agreement. Contrary to what Trump has been claiming, these trade agreements were VERY GOOD for US business and global Multi-national companies (MNCs) in general – the people that they hurt were laborers and workers who lost their jobs or lost their bargaining power when they were very easily replaced by workers in other nations. US companies have used these trade agreements to their advantage to lower labor employment (and hence costs), increase their profits, and have the upper hand over labor. The companies have used this advantage to pretty much demolish the power of the unions. They have also been able to reduce their environmental compliance costs, as many of the nations where the factories were moved to or used, did not have the same level of environmental regulations – so they or the companies that manufactured for them could pollute more in foreign lands, and did not have to worry as much about toxic waste disposal as in the US for these activities.

Some Fundamentals

Most economists argue that "Productivity" is good for the economy. By that they mean **Labor Productivity, or the economic activity per unit of labor**. So if labor used is decreasing then the economy is supposed to be doing well. This is a sure way to job losses and this has happened for the many decades after the second world war. Between 1980 and 2014, the US has lost about 7 million manufacturing jobs. This saves the business owner labor costs, so it increases his or her profits.

Two other productivities are not talked about often. The first is Capital Productivity of the productivity per unit of capital equipment – or how efficient is the expensive capital equipment. The reason this is not talked about, as it is labelled as "Investment", and the government totally subsidizes it by allowing Tax depreciation of the equipment in a very short time – essentially making it free for the business owner. If the capital equipment saves labor, then it again increases profits and capital "costs" never show up as they are "investments". So the government and the financial system is favoring machine over man, and increasing the domination and control of the owner over employees. The following article by Gabriel Horowitz describes how, "The Government Perversely Encourages Machine Over Human Capital", March 28, 2017. For convenience, the link is provided here again.

https://www.forbes.com/sites/washingtonbytes/2017/03/28/how-the-government-perversely-encourages-physical-over-human-capital/#19a8e567f9c6

The other productivity that is seldom talked about is **Energy Productivity** or the economic output per unit of energy consumed. The government subsidizes fossil fuels, so that the energy costs of the business owner are low. So, even if the new capital equipment uses more energy, it is profitable for the business owner to buy it, as the relative costs of energy have been subsidized to be such that it still pays to buy the equipment, pay for more energy consumption, and reduce labor. This often has been a recipe for business owners choosing to be inefficient in energy use, in return for lower labor costs.

If we want good paying manufacturing and productive activity (non-service) jobs to go up, then what we really want is the inverse of Labor Productivity, or let's call it **Employment Generation Efficiency**, or the labor used for each unit of output – the more it is, the more good paying jobs are being created!! There is most probably an optimum where a combination of capital equipment (through semi-automation) and using skill intensive technology and labor, up to which point it pays to hire more people. So, one needs to have a formula to keep encouraging business to hire more people up to a certain point, which can be determined, say, by sales level. A manufacturing engineer can design a factory ten different ways – right now, the design he or she picks is the most highly automated mode that uses expensive capital equipment, because the tax code favors it. Now if the tax code were different, he or she could design the factory in a semi-automated mode using more skilled workers, automating only those parts of the production that clearly create better quality from a semi-automated machine.

The massive tax scam by the Trump tax cut is a total give away to the rich and the robber barons, who it will be proven will not create more good paying jobs. So, the first action must be not only to reverse the tax cut, but also to make sure that for the first time the rich pay their fair share of taxes. Besides that, the tax code needs to be changed to favor pro-employment and pro-environment activity (as emphasized in the section on Jobs and Economy). We need to directly invest in support better and higher paying jobs – much better than Trump and the Republicans can.

Four-Pronged Strategy Proposed for America

1. Pro-Employment Tax Reform: Tax reform that allows depreciation of human capital (training, etc.), and favors greater employment, increasing with the size of the company. Tax reform should be targeted rather than open ended as the Trump Tax cuts, so that they specifically accomplish what is needed.
2. Pro-Employment Industrial Policy: Developing industries systematically that are pro-employment. This would develop industries from R&D to production development, from financing to marketing – pretty much like the US develops Defense industries. Many other nations, from Japan, to Asian Tigers and now China have done this successfully.
3. Local Production for Local Use: Not just Made in America, but local job creation for local consumption. This is the only way that depressed communities can be rejuvenated for the long term. This would encourage R&D and the development of industries that develop capital equipment for the processing of agricultural products – food and non-food, from a wide variety of crops.
4. Transforming All Activities – Making them Sustainable, Pro-Environment & Climate Friendly: By transforming activities leading to sustainable Energy, Cities, Townships, Industry, Transportation, Agriculture, Forestry & Fisheries. Then having massive activities like during the great depression for rejuvenating national ecosystems – forests, wetlands, lakes, rivers, prairies, hills and mountains.

The nations that recovered fastest after World War II were those (many like Japan without raw materials or resources), who had educated, skilled and productive people with a good work ethic. **We have to transform the issues of healthcare and education into economic ones as these are so essential to the quality of the population and their productivity also. So, the issue has to become one of Investing in our people – quality people lead to a quality nation! The nation is great when the people are great – healthy and educated!**

Summary Bullet Points

- INVESTING IN HUMAN CAPITAL – PRO-EMPLOYMENT TAX REFORM
    - Why only depreciate machine capital – depreciate human capital investment too!
    - Not just tax breaks for the rich, and trade policies that increasingly favor pro-employment business
- DEVELOPING INDUSTRIES SYSTEMATICALLY THAT ARE PRO-EMPLOYMENT
    - Not just leaving it to chance
    - Implementing an Industrial Policy to rebuild our industrial base with high employment potential industries
- LOCAL PRODUCTION FOR LOCAL USE – NOT JUST MADE IN AMERICA
    - If companies move manufacturing activity back to the US, companies may benefit, but jobs will not
    - People need to insist that what they consume helps the local economy in terms of jobs – this needs incentives
- TRANSFORMING ALL ACTIVITIES – MAKING THEM SUSTAINABLE
    - Sustainable Energy, Cities, Townships, Industry, Transportation, Agriculture, Forestry & Fisheries

There are many reasons why Trump's strategy on jobs and economy will fail. That's why there is an urgent need to lay out better strategies, that have a better chance of working. Some of this has to do with the anti-employment bias (Tax policy, automation, corporate profit) that has been part of the US economic system for many decades, so that the US has lost 7 million manufacturing jobs between 1980 and 2014.

Trump's strategies to increase good paying (especially manufacturing) jobs are based on trying to get better trade deals, giving companies incentives (or threatening or shaming them) to relocate manufacturing back to the US, reducing taxes on business without corresponding employment generation responsibilities, large infrastructural spending which may temporarily create jobs, greater use of fossil fuels which may again generate a few jobs in coal country, and reducing regulations on businesses and financial companies which let businesses pollute the environment and pocket the profits from lower environmental compliance costs. What actually gets implemented remains to be seen.

The recently enacted Tax cuts for big business, means larger federal deficits which they until recently they had called a big evil (estimated to increase the federal deficit by $1.4 trillion dollars over the next decade), and he and the Republicans are aiming at big increases in military spending (to insane levels – the US already spends more on defense than the next seven nations put together). All of this will mean that the money for big infrastructural spending will be more difficult to find, and they are even talking of cutting Social Security, Medicare and Medicaid. But the companies will pocket the money they get from the tax cuts and run their companies with fewer employees.

In the past, money pumped into the economy (so-called "pump priming") created more business and jobs because it was done in way so as to make sure the money was put in the hands of the poorer parts of the population, who were sure to spend the money, hence increasing the circulation of goods and services in the economy. With Trump's Tax cuts, the companies are going to pocket the money and spend very little of it in new investments (they are not required to do so), and there are much smaller tax cuts for the poorer parts of the population, so the tax cuts will hit the economy with a double whammy – the forced spending by government that occurred in the past will be gone, and only a small portion of the tax cuts will make it back into the economy to compensate for this – this is a sure recipe for a recession!

For a variety of reasons as outlined below, Trump's strategies are bound to fail. **Here are some different strategies that have a higher probability of success in terms of actually creating for the longer term a larger number of better paying jobs for the large numbers of underemployed and underpaid people and workers.**

This article outlines four major strategies for creating more good paying jobs or those that enable people to live reasonably well:

- **Investing in Human Capital – the type of Tax Reform that is really needed by the economy,**
- **An Industrial Policy (as the US does in Defense) that directly invests in and develops industries and businesses with a high employment potential,**
- **Encouraging not just Made in America, but going further to local production for local use that revive local economies where people live and work, and**
- **Applying the principles of Sustainability to ALL human activity – sustainable energy (clean energy – this is already well known and being implemented), sustainable habitats (eco and sustainable cities), sustainable transportation (lower carbon transportation choices), sustainable agriculture, sustainable forestry, sustainable fisheries, and sustainable industry.**

Trump's strategy to create more good paying jobs will fall flat on its face, because it was only intended to create more sales and profits for business. The reason is that business knows how to generate or handle more sales with steady decreases in the numbers of people it employs, and the tax code encourages it – it favors machines over people by providing tax depreciation on capital equipment. **Hence, the only strategies that will work are those that inherently favor more business profit through more**

employment in existing businesses – one method being that of providing tax depreciation for investments in human capital like training and providing other tax incentives for employers to hire more permanent workers.

The other approach is to systematically encourage and develop industry and activity that employ more people per unit of sales – start new businesses or expand existing businesses. What really helps here is a process called **Command Capitalism – government and business cooperating to create success in a category**. Japan used this strategy to build its industrial base after it was totally shattered by World War II, and was able to dominate globally in exports (to name a few - from sewing machines to cars, and cameras to electronics). This strategy has been used by the US defense industry for quite some time (from R&D to production, and financing to marketing) which makes the US succeed globally by all measures in this category. Whether one agrees with this or likes it or not, this makes the US with the country with the most advanced military technologies, and the one with the most success in exports of arms. Only now this approach needs to be applied in employment generating industry.

Getting businesses to move manufacturing operations back from overseas may work a little during the short term, but the difference in labor rates between developed and developing nations is difficult to overcome, unless the government makes it difficult for businesses to import the goods back for sales in the US, or imposes punitive tariffs or custom taxes on imports. Encouraging just US based production, is not enough, what is needed is mainly **local production for local use** - especially empowering and enabling the **local growth and processing of agricultural, forest and fishery products by smaller local businesses.**

At the same time, for the increased employment activity not to be environmentally damaging, it needs to have the principles of environmental sustainability embedded in them – and this may provide added opportunities for employment. There is ample evidence that creating more good paying jobs at the expense of our environment, and while damaging the planet, is a bad long-term strategy. We suggest here an alternative strategies that have a higher probability of generating good paying jobs in a manner that is environmentally sustainable, or in most cases, may be environmentally favorable! So favoring **Sustainable Economic Progress** might be the best way to develop jobs and activities that are good for our future.

Lastly, the minimum basic needs of the entire population need to be met. These are not giveaways – what the American people need is a system and government that make sure that everyone has the opportunity to contribute in a job or business situation to earn their basic minimum needs. We need to raise the minimum wage in the whole nation, so that people that work can afford to have a minimum basic standard of living – no more sweatshops in the nation or in the world. No company should pay anyone for 40 hours of work a week that does not enable them to afford a minimum standard of living – and be able to afford housing, food, clothing and healthcare, in the area where they live.

Here is vision of the four strategies in much more detail.

Strategy #1 – Invest in Human Capital

So, what I say is - If you want to be subsidizing Capital Equipment by eliminating its purchase cost, and calling it an investment, then if you really want better paying jobs, **Invest in Human Capital** – or training, education and skills development of people. Then offer tax depreciation of investments in human capital and reduce the tax depreciation of capital equipment. In other words, tax reform or change in the tax code to make it more profitable to hire and train people, and less profitable to fully automate processes.

The principal reason why business owners may still not like this because of the question of ownership. You see, if a business owner buys capital equipment he owns it and controls it. If he hires and trains people, the hires or employees own the human capital (knowledge, training, skills, etc.), and can walk out with it at any time. One way to make sure a business owner benefits is to have a clause when he trains people that ensures that they work at least for, say, 2 years after the completion of training or education.

Another reason why a tax depreciation on Human Capital Investment is the US national interest is that currently, business has a very hard time finding highly skilled people with the right knowledge and training. Businesses rely on getting such people for free (i.e. not pay for their training before they get hired), or they steal them from other countries (through innovative visa programs). **America is suffering and is less competitive because of this.** One of the nations that systematically encourages human capital investment, either directly or through industry programs, is Germany, and look how well it is doing in Europe. Germany has more coop programs, and they pursue a policy of apprenticeship so that workers become apprentices to highly skilled workers, so that the latter can pass on their practical knowledge to the new hires. So, it is in the US national interest, economically and strategically to be encouraging a more highly skilled people and workforce. **Educational institutions should not be the only ones developing human capital. I actually learned more on the job than when I was getting my Ph.D. degree.** Also, it is time that business pays for what it benefits from. And, it is the type of Tax Reform that US business really needs if it is to be encouraged to generate more jobs!!

Strategy #2 – An Industrial Policy to Create Jobs

The best example of a successful industrial policy in the US is the Defense Industry. Here, the US Government has adopted a systematic approach to weapons development and its related production technology. It goes all the way from ideas generation – by funding independent research and development ideas, to laboratory prototypes, to proof-of-concept prototypes, to pre-production prototypes, to production prototypes, to pilot scale production, to full production. Both to the US armed forces and to foreign governments, much money is spent in marketing, advertising, funding, financing, and after sales support. For better or for worse, there might be a few hundred weapon systems under development in the US at a particular time. The result – the most advanced weapons technologies that are sought by all governments all over the world.

This type of an approach has been called Command Capitalism – that is, Government and Industry cooperating to provide technological and financial success. This approach was used by Japan to lift itself up from essentially a shattered third world level nation to a developed nation able to compete with America. Japan's Ministry of International Trade and Industry (MITI) implemented an Industrial Policy that led to the coordinated development of all aspects of Japanese Trade and Industry, guiding and helping many Japanese industries in the 1950s and the 1960s, according to Wikipedia, not along the lines of a planned economy, but "provided industries with administrative guidance and other direction, both formal and informal, on modernization, technology, investments in new plants and equipment, and domestic and foreign competition." Basically it led to Japanese industry becoming very competitive internationally, and led to both economic growth and jobs in industry. This same Command Capitalism approach was then copied by the "Asian Tigers" – South Korea, Taiwan, Malaysia, and Singapore to develop themselves from developing countries to becoming reasonably advanced. All of these were helped no doubt by the anti-communism encouragement and preferential trade treatment by the US during that time. This same approach is being used in a coordinated fashion by China as it has developed rapidly recently.

What can this mean for the US? Well, it needs to use a similar approach by defining the industries where jobs can be created and systematically helping them in the following way. It needs to analyze which industries and activities have the potential for generating the most jobs, and help develop them all the way from R&D (research and development) to technology development, to help with plants and equipment, financing and marketing. It needs to essentially set up a department or sub-department that basically acts somewhat like MITI and helps facilitate and encourage this whole activity to get off the ground. This will no doubt meet with resistance from current organized industry, whose competitiveness and profits may be threatened, and also economic pundits wedded to the Laissez faire or so-called "free market" approach that the US has followed in all areas except Defense. In a "free market" approach, the government actually favors the big guys and lets them gobble up the little ones (note the current feverish level of merger activity), shedding lots of jobs along the way with mergers, and increased efficiency!! It's about time that the US developed an Industrial Policy that takes up and encourages an alternative industrial policy of the type described above, in an organized fashion!! Only such an approach will reverse the hollowing out of the industrial base of the US and restore its industrial preeminence. Also, many more manufacturing jobs would be created for the long term than otherwise.

As a part of this strategy, **Trade agreements need to be renegotiated, or new trade agreements need to be negotiated that strengthen environmental and labor rights.** Environmental regulations in the US should not be eliminated as they are what have cleaned up America's environment after the industrial "revolution" – but there need to be regulations that are applied globally so that everyone has a level playing field. Tax laws and other incentives should be put in place that favor companies to keep their manufacturing operations in the US, encourage them to manufacture more in the US, and especially in areas where the government has influence, strengthen the Made in America provisions, as the Obama administration had done, which Trump is falsely boasting that only he has done. This should be accompanied by strong measures that encourage exports by financing, helping and enabling companies to export more and have higher export competitiveness, and help export oriented companies by providing support to their infrastructure (electricity, roads, access to ports, raw material supply, transportation, financing, help with marketing, capital equipment supply, R&D and technology development at Universities, etc.) – this can be part of the new Industrial Policy outlined above. Many companies do this type of technology and industrial development – now the government needs to encourage entrepreneurship that fosters this type of pro-employment and pro-environment industrial development.

Strategy #3 – Local Production for Local Use

Trump has been promoting a "Made in America" slogan, which appears to favor things made within the country. However, this approach will not create enough good paying jobs as companies will take advantage of the increased local production, but with fewer people – that's what they have done over the last 40-50 years. There needs to be a further localization of this strategy if it is to produce enough good paying jobs and activities. When people consume today, say cookies, these might be made at one factory and distributed all over the world. By using automated economies of scale at one site may be efficient, but then spending energy for the transportation to distribute this worldwide is very energy wasteful, and one that certainly does not employ many people – and is bad for climate change. Also, the factory also buys the agricultural raw material mainly from large agri-business, which again employs very few people. So if one wants more good employment, then when people consume locally, they should be able to see that their communities and local people are benefitting from local production. In short, if you don't create jobs locally, you have no business selling locally!

This would hurt businesses that are making things at one spot in the world and marketing globally. Sure they use economies of scale, but that is because of capital equipment depreciation (which is a subsidy), and fossil fuel subsidy for transporting the goods. For many high tech items this may be suitable, as the expertise to manufacture these high tech items may be scarce. **However, the big businesses we really need are those that make the machinery for small businesses to manufacture these goods locally all over the place. In short, they would earn their money by being the capital equipment suppliers for small businesses that would use locally grown raw materials, local labor and market locally.** This is an excellent way of creating businesses and jobs in many of the communities where people live.

Economies of scale, marketing and advertising advantages, and food safety concerns favor large scale food plants that process and package at one location, and sell in other states or export to other countries. However, if there is food contamination in one processed and packaged product, it can cause a food safety and public health outbreak throughout the country or even in other nations where the food is exported. This is a case for developing local and regional food hubs, where locally grown foods (especially organic and of many varieties) can be brought by local farmers and local processors of the crops from local farmers. The place where these will be of advantage, is when there are many varieties of a crop, organically grown, rather than the mono-culture of large scale farming of only one "high yielding" or GMO modified crop. For a description of local and regional food systems see: http://www.sustainabletable.org/254/local-regional-food-systems.

There needs to be R&D and development of capital equipment industries that manufacture capital equipment that can be used by small scale processors of agricultural products – food and non-food. The process needs to be supported from agriculture, to harvesting, local processing using this capital equipment (either by farmer or by small processor in local town), development food/agricultural hub where food can be brought to market, and guidance and assistance in financing all along the way. The small businesses need to be helped implement and operate food safety practices, so that big business does not get a chance of winning the fight to get rid of them. This needs to be accompanied by advertising and promotion on a regional and national scale (possibly even global), of this approach. This also needs to be supported by a social and political movement that says, "If local businesses and people are not getting benefitted by more good paying jobs and earnings, then I will not buy it. I will boycott food and agricultural products made by large scale processors that are not based on local processing and employment".

This will also reduce the energy spent in transportation of processed produce all over the nation and through trade all over the world. It would even reduce the carbon footprint of the processing and distribution of agriculture based products. The only products that would be traded would be large scale commodity crops – grains, beans, essential minerals, etc.

Strategy #4 – Innovating to Sustainability in All Activities

Another big opportunity is applying the principles of environmental sustainability as we have come to understand it. The most well-known definition of Sustainability comes from the Brundtland Commission Report of 1987 which stated that: "Sustainable development is development that meets the needs of the present without compromising the ability of future generations to meet their own needs." **My own definition, "Sustainability is that which restores and rejuvenates the conditions that favor life on the** planet." So I am advocating an upgrade from Sustainable development to Rejuvenating development – from Sustainability to Rejuvenability! – to coin a new term! On the flip side, unsustainability is that which destroys or degrades the conditions that favor life on this planet, including ourselves.

Applying the principles of Sustainability, or better yet, to Rejuvenability, to ALL human activity – sustainable energy (clean energy – this is already well known), sustainable habitats (eco and sustainable cities, towns, villages and homesteads), sustainable transportation, sustainable industry (low carbon transportation choices), sustainable agriculture (more organic, with fewer expensive and environmentally damaging inputs), sustainable forestry (which extracts only as much timber so as to leave the ecosystem services of the forest mostly intact), sustainable fisheries (that rejuvenates the fishery and coastal ecosystems, and modifies the catch to enable the fisheries to recover), and sustainability applied to all other activities.

It is now well known that the carbon emissions of all human activity need to be brought to a lower level, to stabilize down to some plateau. **The higher the concentration of carbon dioxide and other greenhouse gases in the atmosphere, the lower the plateau will need to be. That is why the delay being caused by Trump is such a disaster.** But it does not have to be if a different strategy was pursued. We can get to those carbon reductions by what I have been calling the 60:20:20 solution. 60% carbon reductions through energy efficiency, 20% carbon reductions through renewable energy (wind, solar and hydro), and 20% through recycling carbon (either through non-agricultural biofuels or like generating ethanol from factory or power plant exhaust stacks containing carbon dioxide.

Energy efficiency is estimated to be the biggest mine in terms of reducing energy demand and reducing energy costs. It needs to be pursued in all areas – retrofitting all houses and buildings, **making it**

mandatory that ALL new homes and buildings have not only a high standard for energy efficiency, which may include geothermal or heat pumps, but also generate more energy than they consume (by solar and wind power). All new transportation – cars, trucks, buses, locomotives, planes – should have higher and higher mandatory fuel efficiency standards. Most of these should be converted to the electric mode with on board batteries or electric wire connected drives – with the electricity all provided by renewable sources of energy. All of these activities should be developed and encouraged – with new energy efficiency technologies, especially for houses and buildings creating the most jobs.

It is now well known that solar, wind and hydro energy generation have created many more jobs than nuclear or fossil fuel energy generation activities, and are capable of generating many more jobs – both in installation and in operation. In 2016, the number of people employed in solar energy were 374,000 or 43% of the total people employed in power generation field, wind energy employed 101,738 people, and coal, gas and oil combined employed only 187,000 people or only about 23% of the total. Coal mining employment reached a peak and now only employs 53,000 people, and oil and gas extraction reached a peak and by mid-2016 employed 388,000 people. A report by the Environmental Defense Fund indicated that solar jobs were growing at a rate 12 times faster than for the rest of the economy. The wind sector added 32% more jobs in 2015-2016, and solar sector added 25% more jobs in the same period. Energy efficiency employment increased by 9% in this period, and about 198,000 more people were expected to be hired in 2017. See the article in the link below.

http://spectrum.ieee.org/energywise/energy/renewables/for-us-jobs-creation-renewables-are-a-better-bet-than-coal

All of this goes to show that Clean Energy (renewable energy and energy efficiency) has added and can continue to add many more jobs than other sectors of the economy – especially the fossil fuel sector. So, more good paying jobs are created by investing more in solar and wind than investing more in coal and oil.

The next big opportunity is that of transforming our cities, towns, villages and homesteads or establishing new ones that are **Sustainable Habitats** – what this means is explained below. It does not take a rocket scientist to figure out that our cities, worldwide, have been very poorly and inefficiently designed and are often wasteful of energy and materials, and damaging to the environment. And they do not provide safe and clean conditions – with often the air and water being very polluted. **As per Wikipedia an Eco-city or Sustainable City is one that follows the principles of environmental sustainability (so that the environment or nature around them has been able to sustain itself), functions as a zero-carbon city (net zero carbon emissions), produces all of its energy from renewable sources, functions like an ecosystem in terms of recycling its wastes (my interpretation), and lives in harmony with all types of life.** So, the type of infrastructural development should be such that there are areas set aside for these activities co-located near to each other – the production of renewable energy, the growth and sale of agricultural produce, the treatment and recycling of waste (compost, water treatment, etc.) and the treatment and recycling of water. This is the type of infrastructural development that we really need – not spending more and more on supporting the fossil fuel powered transportation.

Urban sprawl that relies on the automotive mode of transportation mainly should be banned, and all new developments should be built on the basis of eco or sustainable city criteria.

For **Sustainable Transportation** the city is suitably planned to maximize the use of walking, biking and public transportation. **My interpretation of this also is that the city be designed so as minimize the distances needing to be travelled, and hence**

reducing the distances that cars need to travel, and discourage the use of car transportation – both to relieve congestion and to reduce the carbon emissions from vehicles. The design of the city would be such as to maximize the areas in which the people could walk and bike and take public transportation, and minimize the use of transportation needing fossil fuel combustion – hence minimizing noise, pollution and carbon emissions from vehicular travel. The transportation plan for the habitat must offer quiet, clean, healthy and safe low carbon choices – also ones that are suitable for the elderly and the disabled. Transforming our cities to this mode, and creating new developments and cities that do this will create many jobs. **This is the type of infrastructure that we need to invest in – not more and more infrastructure spending on roads and bridges supporting cars and trucks!**

Next let's talk about agriculture. The kind of Green Revolution type agriculture that the US has adopted and taught the rest of the world, is the source of many problems. Besides mechanization that reduced the labor content, this type of farming has led to the growth of large Agri-business farms, has led to the disappearance of small farms and many people have abandoned agriculture as a source of livelihood. It has destroyed a very large number of jobs. From 1870, when 50% of the population was engaged in farming operations, in 2012 only 3.2 million people were engaged in agricultural activity, and there were about 757,900 legally employed agricultural workers. From 1999-2009, about 50% of farm workers were undocumented non-citizens. Jobs in agriculture have disappeared at a fast rate.

This kind of agriculture still uses a lot of land tillage, chemical fertilizer, pesticides, herbicides, irrigation water, diesel fuel, and "high yielding" or GMO (genetically modified organisms) type seeds. It is extremely polluting, very expensive, exhausts the soil relatively fast, and is very expensive. It has tried to save costs by mechanization and reducing the labor content of the operations. Environmentally this type of agriculture has been very damaging, leading to pollution of water bodies (with the biocides) and the remaining fertilizer has caused the growth of algae and the death of lakes. By creating artificial surpluses, this agriculture has depressed prices.

Sustainable Agriculture can reverse this entire trend as well as create more jobs, income and employment in the farm sector. Sustainable agriculture means farming that uses less tillage, more natural fertilizer, none or very little pesticides and herbicides, conserves water, and uses a lot of different types of mostly traditional varieties of seeds and crops. This type of agriculture is more skill intensive, requires more attention to land management, and at the organic end, produces farm output that fetches a far better price. Best of all, it is capable of providing more jobs and batter livelihoods and incomes for more people. A study of 13 Missouri counties showed that converting to sustainable agriculture would provide support for more than 165 farm households per county, and more than 300 additional farm and non-farm households in total. Plus, it would support that local production for local use that was described above, as more other people could earn their income processing the agricultural output. It is the type of revival that rural America desperately needs.
http://web.missouri.edu/ikerdj/papers/sa-cdst.htm

Sustainable Forest Management is another area that can create many jobs. The definition adopted by the international Food and Agricultural Organization (FAO) is: "The stewardship and use of forests and forest lands in a way, and at a rate, that maintains their biodiversity, productivity, regeneration capacity, vitality and their potential to fulfill, now and in the future, relevant ecological, economic and social functions, at local, national, and global levels, and that does not cause damage to other ecosystems." In this approach, resources are harvested from forests (including timber), in a manner that the forest itself is standing and performing much of its ecological function and serving as an important carbon sink. Plantation style forestry that uses clear cutting through mechanized operations, reduces labor content and leaves a devastated countryside. The same is true of the clear cutting of old growth forests. On the other hand, sustainable forest management can create many jobs through afforestation, reforestation, management of existing forests, revival of urban green spaces, improvements of watersheds, protection of forests from fire (or an ecosystem approach) and the growth of forest tourism. Such investments would further revive rural areas and raise their living standards. http://www.fao.org/docrep/012/i1025e/i1025e02.htm

Employment in fishing has been declining for some time now. Employment could be revived if sustainable fishing practices were adopted, as in many cases they are. **Sustainable Fishery Management** means that the fish catch must not exceed the regenerative capacity of the fishery, so that there is enough fish left that enable them to reproduce in sufficient numbers. The marine ecosystems health must improve over time, so that the species that depend on it can reproduce and have a habitat that enables them to survive and thrive. All of the coastal ecosystems of the US needs to be revived as they haven degraded by too much human development – marine coastal ecosystems such as mangrove swamps need to be revived, so that storm surges are lessened and species get habitats to survive in. This may mean in some places giving less importance to beaches and more to the coastal ecosystems. The big advantage will be that hurricanes and coastal storms of the type that Florida and the Carolinas have experienced over the last decade will have their disastrous impact lessened, helping those states economically.

And last but not least, **Sustainable Industry**, which uses mainly renewable raw materials, helps develop alternatives or replacements faster than depleting mined raw materials, has a low carbon footprint, is more skill intensive rather than capital or energy intensive, does not create toxic wastes or effectively treats them, recycles the rest of its wastes, and only sustainably uses resources from carbon sinks (forests, agriculture or fisheries) – so that these do not deplete too fast so as to collapse the ecosystems on which these depend. Also, truly sustainable industry is that which encourages and enables the people involved (management and workers) to be empowered to continuously improve their knowledge and skills, and have full encouragement for their creative and productive skills, conserve capital and energy, and reorient production methods so as to make them interesting, safe and healthy.

Conclusion – Jobs & Economy

I have described how Trump's strategy on jobs and economy is bound to fail, and why this will pollute and damage our environment. In its stead I have proposed a four-part strategy to create more and better jobs in ALL parts of the US economy by tax reform that favors greater employment, an industrial and trade policy that develops and supports employment generating industries, encourages local production for local use (thus reviving the rural areas and small towns that have been devastated), and encourages all human activity to transition to a stronger version of sustainability, investing in the right type of infrastructural development that supports this, thereby making America cleaner, greener, healthier and happier, with more widespread prosperity for all!

Rejuvenating the Environment & Solving Climate Change

We need to overcome the Trump Anti-Planet, Anti-People and Anti-Environment Agenda

- We must get back on track – cleaner America, dedicated to Climate Change actions

- Trump's Actions on Climate Change are destructive. Trump's "Great Leap Backwards" on Climate Change – Effects in each major area
- Effect of Global Warming on the US and the World – How both are ALREADY suffering
  - And it is getting worse!
  - Hurricanes like Harvey will disprove Trump
- We must get back on track with the Paris Agreement
- We have solutions for Climate Change
  - Clean Energy – solar, wind and others
  - Energy Efficiency – everything must be energy efficient
  - Electrify everything and base on renewables
  - Restore & rejuvenate our national and global carbon sinks

On an action basis we have to fight for climate change actions at the state, city and county levels, while pushing coordination and actions at the global level. Biggest on the list have to be low carbon solutions for energy, transportation and housing. The efforts of Nextgen Climate (now Next Gen America), Climate Reality and 350.org are in the forefront when it comes to organizations. Nextgen America and Climate Action Lobby are leading some of the lobbying and political action fronts.

Sierra Club actions like ready for 100 (which a city can adopt in order to transition to 100% renewables) should be encouraged at all cities, as also their action to Buy Clean (which means choosing low carbon options in their purchasing decisions). Specifically, we have to fight actions like those of the Koch Brothers, who fought and defeated a measure that would have favored clean transit and clean transportation. Other actions need to include slowly getting rid of the use of fossil fuels in our economy, by supporting the actions of organizations like Fossil Free California, that seeks get pension funds to divest from fossil fuel companies.

Our inspiring vision has to be one of beautiful, clean, low carbon and rejuvenated America, that provides an inspiring example of how we can transform our nation and our planet back to a beautiful paradise, with clean and organic productivity that provides clean food and raw materials and livelihoods for the new economy!

Trump's action of withdrawing from the Pairs Agreement on Climate Change is, "The Great Leap Backwards". Like Mao's great leap forward, it will fall flat on its face. The US has become the laughing stock of the world. The only two nations who did not sign the Agreement were Syria and North Korea (and now I believe that Syria has signed). Trump has delegated us to the category of rogue outcast nations.

The problem with Trump & Climate Deniers

There are two categories of people who are Climate Deniers: (1) Those who absolutely hate the fact that the fossil fuel based energy reliance of civilization as has existed till now is being questioned, and (2) The people who take the "Tobacco Institute Approach" - where commercial interests like the Tobacco Institute hire scientists to produce data and theories that contradict the mainstream scientific knowledge and consensus - in the case of tobacco, to convince the public that cigarette smoking was not bad for their health! This caused confusion in the mind of the public and delayed action by the politicians on the control of smoking in facilities used by the public.

There have been Climate Deniers who have been ignoring and criticizing most of the other scientists of the world that have seen the evidence of geosphere measurements and have been drawing conclusions that are now mainstream. However, the Trump administration and Climate Deniers come up with their own scientific data and their own methods, none of which have been whetted by other scientists or have been subjected to peer review in globally accepted scientific journals.

The situation gets more serious by the day. The more they are able to delay political action, the higher does the concentration of Carbon Dioxide get in the atmosphere, and the greater would be the carbon reductions needed when the whole world does get serious about effective action. The sooner we would have gotten started after 1992 (see below – Rio de Janeiro global conference when the first Climate Change Treaty was signed), the better the world would be, and a higher level of fossil fuel use could have been stabilized at.

Background on Climate Change & Clean Energy

1. Trump and Climate Deniers do not present any scientific evidence to refute the scientific observation that Green House Gases (GHG) actually warm the atmosphere - of which Carbon Dioxide makes the biggest contribution.

2. Hundreds of scientists, most of whom have contributed to the five IPCC reports since 1992 (Rio Conference when the UN framework Convention (Treaty) on Climate Change - UNFCC was signed by many nations). Each IPCC report has been more and more emphatic in liking man activity (Anthropogenic) contributions to Climate Change. IPCC's first report in early 1990s started out by saying that Climate Change is happening, and that humans are probably contributing to climate Change. Since then, the fact that scientific measurements by NOAA - National Oceanic and Atmospheric Administration, and many other non-US global scientific organizations have concluded that the SCIENTIFIC EVIDENCE is there to conclude that Humans are MOST CERTAINLY contributing to Climate Change. ANY atmospheric chemist or physicist who knows his scientific knowledge, would agree that the

atmospheric physics and chemistry of higher levels of greenhouse gases causing excess warming of the atmosphere, is wholly confirmed and true.

3. Computer models like Global Circulation Models (GCMs) are able to predict much of the general observations of Climate Change. Then, if specific sea temperatures are measured in the Pacific - computer models are able to predict more precisely the severe weather that might occur in a particular year. This usually results in predictions of whether a year will be an El Nino year or an El Nina year – this determines whether the Caribbean and east coast see hurricanes, or whether the west coast gets storms.

4.Trump displays an ignorance of planetary history - of how, over 4.6 billion years, the Earth has cooled from a molten ball, and has gone through many cycles of carbon sequestration of fossils (to form the deposits of oil and coal) which cooled the planet's atmosphere to the point that life as we know it, and the human species, could prosper, evolve and survive. Then came the ice ages over the last few million years. When the last mini ice age lifted about 10,000 years ago, we have had the flowering of most of human civilization as we know it. We are now in the Holocene Interglacial period - we would have been headed for another mini ice age, if it were not for the current human induced global warming.

5.The Climate Change situation is already disastrous globally and, in the US, (order my Personal Climate Change Handbook, Hari Lamba from Amazon - which has detailed the worsening disaster see are already being subjected to - which are getting worse). For the US - worsening hurricanes, tornadoes, extreme rain events, flash flooding, worsening wild fires, worsening coastal storms (like Storm Sandy). India is suffering from worsening heat waves each year, massive rain events (Mumbai (2005), Leh (2011), and Uttarakhand - recently) that lead to catastrophic mudslides and loss of life - these were unheard of events until recently. Have country wide rains that submerge entire nations - Mozambique, Pakistan, etc.). Islands like Maldives are rapidly disappearing under the rising sea - He would not be talking the way if he were a citizen of Maldives.

6.The Ozone crisis was a similar one. Deniers and the chemical industry fought the developing evidence and theory on the depletion of the Ozone layer by CFCs - Chloro-Fluoro-Carbons. Until preliminary evidence by a British scientist working on a low budget in Antarctica led to a NASA expedition and evidence gathering planes were flown by NASA through the Ozone "Hole" that had developed over Antarctica that swung over Australia - this proved the chemical reaction of CFCs and Ozone was actually happening as evidence inside the hole of the resultant chlorine oxide (right hand side of chemical equation) was detected in significant quantities. Then, even an anti-environmental president like Ronald Reagan had to agree for US to sign the Ozone treaty that set in motion the most effective means yet of solving a global environmental problem - the Ozone crisis. We all know that the destruction of the Ozone layer (that was formed when enough oxygen developed), protects life and us from the bad effects of increased ultra-violet light.

7.The fifth and most recent report of the IPCC (intergovernmental Panel on Climate Change - hundreds of Scientists from all over the world), outlines in detail the theory and symptoms of Climate Change, and what needs to be done to avoid its worst consequences and finally solve the problem. The consequences are in terms of rising temperatures (heat waves), droughts (in some regions), and massive rains and flooding in other regions (the massive Mississippi River flood of 2005, flooding in S. Carolina 200x), worsening and stronger hurricanes and cyclones, worsening coastal storms (like storm Sandy) with large storm surges inland, rising sea level rise (2/3rds of Florida and much of Bangladesh will be under water by the end of this century.

8.Global Actions: In December 2015, thanks to the leadership of Obama and the US, almost all of the actions of the world signed the

Paris Agreement, where for the first time they agreed to work together (voluntarily to begin with) to begin to reduce their carbon emissions. The only nations who did not sign were Syria and North Korea. Trump's action of making us withdraw from the Paris accord has cast us in with rogue nations and has greatly reduced US standing in the world. The US is militarily the most powerful nation in the world, and spends more than at least the next seven nations - and its strength is not governed by the fact that it has reduced its carbon emissions. In fact, withdrawal of the US from the Paris agreement weakens our standing with our Allies, who are one of the major reasons for our global military strength.

A Bold program on Climate Change & Our Environment to Defeat Trump on Climate Change

We need to fight Trump's agenda on Climate Change and the pollution of our environment by proposing a bold action on Climate change, to be implemented after Trump is defeated. The Solutions are also well laid out and are shown to be within practical grasp, given the global political will. Solar and Wind energy have come a long way. The cost of Wind energy is now less than that for coal for generating electricity, they are actually creating more good paying jobs than either oil, coal or natural gas per unit.

Besides Oil, coal, and even natural gas are very polluting - coal being the worst - it generates more carbon dioxide per BTU (British Thermal Unit - unit of energy) than any other energy source.

It took many decades of the Clean Air Act and the Clean Water Act to clean up what was a very polluted United States - the Great Lakes were very polluted and thanks to these actions are much cleaner now, making much of the water to be easily used for drinking after normal water treatment processes. Solar and Oil give zero pollution in their operational modes, and hence are clean energy modes. Commercially, for Solar and Wind, the "Fuel" or energy is free - you do not have to pay anyone for them. Maybe, that is the reason the fossil fuel industry does not like them, as they can make more profits by mining and selling fossil fuels. Also, they are the true way to energy independence - we need not be dependent commercially or strategically on oil from oil producing countries. So Clean Renewable Energy is of great advantage from security, energy and environmental reasons - plus, when combined with energy efficiency, provide us with solutions to the problem of Climate Change.

Strengthening Women's Rights

No nation can be great if the women are not empowered, equal and rewarded in every way so as to be able to contribute to the greatness of the nation. It is the time in history that women should have full social, political, legal, financial, medical and employment rights. There is little doubt now that the rights of women have to be promoted to the point that they are equal individually or as partners in ALL matters.

Also, as the Me Too movement has illustrated so well, the time has come when the harassment and victimization of women to end. All relationships should be consensual, even between spouses or other similar formal and informal relationships. No man should ever attempt to sexually harass or engage in behavior that victimize a girl or woman, physically, mentally, financially, psychologically or sexually. All of society, and especially elected officials, media people, and companies should have strong programs to educate people and always have effective means of dealing with problems when they arise. Every girl or woman should have the access to recourse if and when she is harassed. Although the same applies when men are being harassed, the special needs of women should be addressed effectively. While problems should be sought to be resolved amicably at lower levels of harassment, punishment should be effective when needed.

Violence against women either in society, in companies or in the military should not be tolerated. As the National Organization of Women emphasizes, all aspects of violence against women must be fully addressed, namely, "domestic violence; sexual assault; sexual harassment; violence at abortion clinics; hate crimes across lines of gender, sexuality and race; the gender bias in our judicial system that further victimizes survivors of violence; and the violence of poverty emphasized by the radical right's attacks on poor women and children — all of which result from society's attitudes toward women and efforts to "keep women in their place."

There is no doubt that one of the primary ways of achieving full rights for women, should be the passing of the Equal Rights Amendment (ERA) to the US Constitution. Only one more state needs to ratify the amendment and it will become law. Together with the avoidance of harassment, this should be at the top of the list. Economic equality is also important in jobs, housing, business and finances. Women must have total control of their bodies and health. In this respect they must have full rights and access to reproductive freedom, birth control, and abortion (when needed). Women should have the full freedom to make all decisions relating to their reproductive health in consultation with their doctors.

Stronger Gun Control & Reducing Gun Violence

Gun violence has become a national epidemic, and even children are no longer safe in their schools. The main issues that gun control advocates are fighting for are the expansion and tightening of background checks; the inability of criminals, mental health sufferers, terrorist list people, etc. to buy guns; the banning of assault weapons; abolishment of bump stocks; reduction of concealed carry laws; the expansion of mental health care; and greater responsibility of gun owners to keep their guns from being misused by others.

A vision that would be very beneficial for America is gun control to the point that there is a reduction of gun violence, some middle ground so that guns rights advocates can keep some guns for self-protection, and a national program to deal with mental health, anger management and social alienation. It would be good if there can be some middle ground in the whole situation of gun rights, gun control and gun violence. This will not happen until the influence of the National Rifle Association (NRA) and other gun rights groups is diminished so that some sanity can be restored to this issue. Maybe a revision of the Second Amendment that clearly specifies what rights individuals have to possess guns, and conditions (mental health, etc.) under which they cannot possess guns. If gun rights folks want to engage in sporting activity and to protect themselves, then one hand gun and one shot gun, both properly registered and controlled, should do it – why any more than that?

One of the most promising things that has happened recently has been the activism of the students of the Parkland College in Florida, after which many students around the country have been energized. This bodes well for democracy in America if these young folks can be energized, motivated, and activated, not just for gun control, but also for all the issues addresses in this manual and the accompanying book. These students need to unite, not only with other gun control organizations but also with other movements and organizations described in this manual – because the same people and organizations who are fighting for other issues, are also fighting for gun control.

Strengthening the Fabric of Our Society - Diversity

The vision here for America is that all citizens must be first class citizens! The best thing that can happen for the nation, that every person, regardless of color, race, religion, national origin, gender or sexual orientation should feel this way and be treated this way, not only socially, but in all matters, and especially in the criminal justice system. The criminal justice system needs a massive overhaul – the police, the judiciary and the detention system. There have been many attempts at a dialogue that would help improve relations between the police and minority communities of color.

The vision here is the following: The relations between police and the community have to improve, there needs to be respect and dialogue on both sides, persons stopped by police should behave respectfully, and push comes to shove, police must not use excessive force, except when they are being fired upon. We need to stop arming the police with military level hardware. The judicial system and laws of sentencing need to be reformed so that the bail, and imprisonment laws do not produce long imprisonment for minor non-violent crimes, and the main focus of the judicial system (like the Scandinavian countries) should be rehabilitation, education and job orientation, and help with job placement and transition, so that people coming out of prison make it successfully out of prison and do not go back to criminal activity or imprisonment.

Being tough on crime has unfortunately meant to be tough on blacks and Latin Americans. That is why the prisons are full of people from these two communities, and the US spends too much on prisons and has the highest number of prisoners of any developed country. The new vision will mean that the funds will be spent on education, training and job placement in depressed communities of any color, and this includes depressed white and native American communities.

Background on Diversity

It is now known that native Americans had migrated to and lived in the Americas for the last 10,000-30,000 years. In the last 500 years, wave after wave of European migration populated North America, and out of this migration, suppression and displacement of native Americans, import of slaves from Africa, and the struggle against colonial rule led to the formation of the United States of America. As many of the migrants were escaping religious persecution in Europe, the founding fathers made sure that religious freedom was enshrined into the constitution and that there was separation between church and state – this avoided many of the abuses of the use of organized religion in politics that had been seen in Europe for hundreds of years. Between the two world wars, Franklin Roosevelt was instrumental in national policies that helped the nation avoid the political extremes of communism and fascism – this was very fortunate for the US, as it produced great national strength that helped it win the war. After the second world war, the nation encouraged the migration from most of the countries of the world, and this brought another wave of migration, and today the US has people from all over the world.

Many nations have shown that a nation's strength and vitality are driven by the ability to listen to all of the different points of view, and try to include and involve all parts of society in national life. This is actually the very basis of democracy – the true way of providing power to the people, if democracy is properly defined – Trump's way shakes up the current establishment but leads to dictatorial trends. Nations have prospered when they have listened to and accommodated all segments of society – they have been internally and externally at peace. This has been true even when the nation is dominated by one race and one religion. A clear example where the opposite trend led to situations that were bad for the nation and bad for the world is Nazi Germany. That approach took that nation and the world on the primrose path to hell. Fascist Italy and Imperial Japan were other examples that led to severe problems for themselves and others.

The strength of the United States of America is that the whole world looks up to it and wants to be part of it, or cooperate with it. People from every nation in the world can be found here. After World War II, the nation truly opened up to the world, and now people from all over the world have contributed to its progress.

Immigration policy for the most part led to intelligent, educated and productive people to migrate to the US – often leading to brain drain from other Nations. Some parts of the immigration policy did not always include qualified people – such as family reunification aspects. On the other hand, US agriculture has prospered from the migration from Mexico of farm labor that ensured that crops were harvested and got to the market in a timely fashion. Rather than this producing illegal immigration, it would be better for the nation if it found a way for Mexicans and others from Latin America to come and work legally in the US, returning to their home countries when they are done (which many of them want to do anyway).

It is false to say that whites have suffered from reverse discrimination as the white supremacist groups claim. A look around the country, the congress and the corporate sector, clearly show that whites overwhelmingly dominate the scene. This has not been a bad thing, as white America has accommodated and been cooperative with people of other races and national origins. This has led to a healthy and happy situation, where people of all races, religions and national origins have been welcomed, made to feel at home, and empowered and enabled to contribute to making America greater than it is.

America can be portrayed as a mosaic or as a melting pot – actually it is both. Either way, it helps America to be getting the benefit of the world's languages, cultures and religions without actually travelling elsewhere. When one immigrates to the US, there are some core values that one gets to feel are American – hard work, entrepreneurship, fairness, equality, treating people with respect, freedom of thought, freedom of expression (with limits), democracy, respect for the constitution, getting ahead based on competency and contribution, helping each other, and helping the world. When immigrants contribute to these values, they are entering the melting pot, and when they bring good values and cultures from their own countries, they are contributing to the mosaic. What they need to avoid are combining the worst values from their home countries with the worst tendencies among segments in America (discrimination, gun violence, sexual exploitation, etc.).

If one talks about the rights of ownership, all of the land of all of the Americas was "owned" by Native American tribes. They were here for at least more than 10,000 years before the coming of Europeans. If one is to talk about ownership, there needs to be some justice and respect for our Native American brothers. They have taught us how to look after the land in a sustainable fashion – the ecology of North America was in very good condition and the eco-systems were vibrant and man and nature lived in harmony.

African Americans have come a long way from the time they were brought over as slaves. Abraham Lincoln and the Northern United States fought for and won the American Civil War in order to free the African Americans. Today, they are integrated in every aspect of American life, including the military. Early on, Jesse Owens shamed Hitler by winning in athletics at the 1936 Munich Olympics – immediately showing that no race is superior to another. The only way forward is for the race relations to be based on goodwill, fairness and justice. Latin Americans similarly are integrated in all aspects of American life and provide a bridge to Latin America. Besides that, a well-managed relationship with Mexico means that our nation south of the border will continue to be our strong ally. When many wait and painstakingly work through legal channels to migrate to or visit America, illegal immigration is bad, US borders should be strictly controlled (as people from all countries of the world have used the southern border to illegally enter the US), and those who over stay their visas should be firmly dealt with. But the problem of so many immigrants (especially farm labor from Mexico, or those who have been here for many years) that are here illegally should be handled more imaginatively.

All minorities, who are basically from all the nations of the world, provide a bridge to these nations and provide help in interpretation and in business links. Our diversity, of thought, ideas, races, ethnicities, national origins and sexual orientations – and respect for and encouragement of these strengthen our nation. Trying to sanitize this nation at this stage of the history and to try to make it one uniform race and one religion (maybe one branch only of Christianity), will be disastrous for America and will lead us and the world into chaos and violence. It will not produce the kind of economic benefits, golden age or a Great America, that the white supremacists hope for, and which Trump champions.

Vision for Our Tribal Nations

Native Americans are the original Americans before Europeans came to this land. Throughout history they have been victimized, displaced, herded and even whole tribes have been exterminated. However today, they are facing situations that are much worse with low levels of healthcare, economic development, education, housing and law enforcement. At the same time they suffer much from crime by non-Indians and suffer much at the hands of the external criminal justice system, while they do not have enough control and jurisdiction over their areas.

The time has come for some justice and for taking care of our native American peoples. Bernie Sanders has tried to do much for the Tribal nations, and this vision is based on initiatives and programs for them, as described on his website "Our Revolution". We have to begin with the process of supporting tribal sovereignty and tribal jurisdictions, in upholding the letter and the spirit of treaties, expanding consultation with them to find solutions, protecting their sacred places and cultures, and restoring tribal lands from the use of which they have been alienated. Then we need to invest in improving education (keeping in view that this must include teaching of their languages and cultures – full funding of Bureau of Indian Education), advancing economic development (for job opportunities, business development and infrastructure), improving housing (funding of Indian Housing Block Grant Program), and improving healthcare (full funding of the Indian Health Service).

At the same time, when native Americans live outside reservations, they must have full voting rights so they can participate fully politically in American society. Racial bias and discrimination against native American people must be ended and the use of sports mascots from their cultures in all school, college and commercial sports teams must be ended. For a people that did such a good job of ecologically preserving the environment of the Americas, it is ironic that their areas are suffering so much from climate change and environmental degradation. Not only must environmental restoration programs be undertaken in their areas in consultation with and in cooperation with tribal nations (it has been recognized globally that indigenous people have much wisdom and knowledge of ecological management), but the practice of routing oil pipelines through their land areas must be ended. We must finally begin the process of respectfully and purposefully helping our native American brothers and sisters to sustainably begin to use their wisdom and all the knowledge and resources out there, to help them to begin to have a good and healthy life – we owe it to them. It will help them and strengthen our nation.

Reforming our Immigration Strategy and System

The only original inhabitants who migrated to North America thousands of years ago, are the Native Americans, the tribal nations. In addition, the Africans who were brought here as slaves came forcibly against their will. Before independence, immigrants came when they wanted to, although the British must have regulated their coming, and many of the white immigrants brought by the British or rich residents were indentured laborers. The rest of the population are all relatively recent immigrants. So, in that sense, the United States of America is a land of immigrants. Most of those who landed after independence were essentially illegal and they came and were processed and became residents – the Irish, the Germans, the Italians, and the Scandinavians all came in this way.

The system of legal immigration from the 1950s on were first and foremost based on education and skills that the US either lacked or had in short supply – engineers, doctors, technicians, software programmers, etc. In this way, the US benefitted a great deal from educated and skilled people migrating here and making the US more competitive than it would have been otherwise, and by providing essential services. This was not true of family reunification cases, where relatives of the original educated and skilled migrants, were not necessarily so highly educated or skilled. Still, overall, the US benefitted from this process, although the nations from where these people came complained of brain drain.

On the other hand, the waves of illegal immigrants, mainly from Central and South America, has led to the problem that we have today. Many argue that these folks are needed, because there are many jobs requiring manual labor which other US citizens just will not do, for example, farm labor. The counter argument is that these people take away much needed jobs and hence worsen the jobs and economic situation for other Americans. Also, there appears to be a fear among some that immigrants from Islamic nations will cause social and security problems. Another fear among some segments of the white population is that all of this legal and illegal will lead to a situation where whites are in minority, and hence will become politically and economically disadvantaged.

The vision that we propose here takes some from the recent efforts at immigration reform with some new ideas. In 2013, the Senate passed an immigration bill that was approved by 62 senators but the house even refused to take it up for discussion. The vision listed below is based mainly on that bill. First, legal immigration should predominantly be based on skills and education that are in short supply in the US – like before, if not enough Americans are being educated in that field, or if people of higher education and skills are needed. Family reunification is still important for many US Citizens, but the number of visas available for this should be reduced, and only unmarried children under the age of 31 should be allowed. Temporary H-1 work visas for highly skilled workers (engineers, computer scientists and programmers) should be kept at current levels if US companies are to be competitive with foreign based companies. For low skilled workers, like farm laborers, of which there is a severe shortage, the US should have an expanded work visa type program, that allows workers to come and work in the US for certain lengths of time, as long as they go back to their countries and maintain residency elsewhere, with no voting or citizen rights here – this would solve problems on both sides of the border with Mexico. For illegal or undocumented young people who are currently covered by the DACA program, should be allowed to become legal permanent residents within a one-year period. All other illegal or undocumented immigrants should be allowed to continue to stay in the US and work legally, for say a 10 year period, after which they should be allowed to apply for and receive legal permanent resident status. The time period by which these immigrants can become citizens for those two categories should be either 6 or 16 years.

Truly Strengthening our Defense & Promoting A Peaceful and Cooperative World

Military Power, Policing, US Interests, the US Budget and World Peace

Trump is weakening US Defense by damaging the very pillars on which US military might depends – he has alienated our allies, he has engaged in irresponsible rhetoric against North Korea (making that situation much worse), he has engaged in irresponsible rhetoric in fighting Terrorism (making it a religious crusade – playing into the hands of terrorists), he has politicized the military which is having a bad effect on the morale of the military, and he has very little credibility with the military commanders (there has even been talk of not obeying illegal commands issued by him).

There is little doubt that the US defense forces are the strongest is the world, and there have been many factors that have contributed to its superiority. It is false for Trump to say that Obama neglected the US military or that it is weak. The defense budget grew steadily under Obama and then remained steady, and he did not engage in the unwise and costly boondoggles such as the Iraq war initiated by Bush, that ended up creating such a mess. **Obama very wisely and courageously built up the strength of the US military, rebuilt strong cooperation with US allies and security partners, and kept the adversaries under check. Trump has foolishly weakened our relationships with US allies, weakened our alliance with NATO, spoiled relationships with Australia, done absolutely nothing to check ISIS, and weakened our economic relations (and hence our security ties), talked about re-opening the nuclear arms race (he asked for a ten-fold increase in nuclear weapons) with the Pacific rim nations. His is the kind of foolish bluster that only foolish dictators engage in.** His sectarian approach to the middle-east with calls for fight against "radical Islamic terrorism", plays well to his support base that is Islamophobic, but only worsens the danger globally and domestically with extreme terrorists that misuse Islam. Meanwhile, he is attempting to politicize the military, which is bad for that powerful establishment and its current total support for the US Constitution.

There are some in America who question the need for a powerful military and claim that it is not a force for good in the world, and feel that the money would be much better spent improving the lives of its people. They point to the support of the US of many powerful and tyrannical dictators, the undue interference in the affairs of other nations, and the protection of its own financial interests. That said, it is false for Trump to say that the US has not acted in its own interests – the US approach, while taking account of the shared interests with its allies has generally acted in its own self-interest. But the claim has always been that the US is acting in the best interests of the world, and hence has been able to maintain the moral high ground in its rhetoric. Be that as it may, the rich and the powerful in the US have traditionally looked for a powerful military, that for its own security and economic interests should dominate the world and project its military might globally. This originated from the former US President Andrew Jackson and hence is called the Jacksonian approach. The approach originating from Woodrow Wilson, which is called the Wilsonian approach tries to take the moral high road with stress on human rights and democracy. This kind of rationale led to the Iraq war.

The strength of US Defense comes from a good number of factors:

1. **US Defense Budget** is at least higher than the next seven nations combined. Contrary to claims, the US budget kept increasing during the Obama years. The part of the budget that is devoted to fighting wars is significant. Increasing the budget further does not make sense. Getting NATO nations to spend more for their own defense and not burden the US excessively may be a good approach (the US contributes to about 70% of the NATO budget).

2. **Weapons Systems:** The US has developed and continues to develop more advanced weapons systems than the other nations – there is NO nation that can stand up to US weapons technology. Russia has resumed its advanced weapons development as it did in the Soviet days, but it has a lot of catching up to do, and its defense budget is about 10-15% of the US budget. China is catching up but still is not quite there yet. China has spent much on developing its capabilities, but its capabilities are local and regional – it is not prepared or equipped to project its power globally, but present a challenge to the US in the western Pacific.

3. **Nuclear Weapons:** The only nation that is capable of devastating the US with nuclear weapons is Russia. That is what needs attention. US nuclear weapons technology is aging and need of modernization – the US military is paying attention to these, as well as innovative and qualitative improvements in its nuclear weapons. North Korean nuclear capabilities are tiny compared to the US or even other nuclear nations – the danger is mainly local and regional, and in regard to the proliferation of nuclear weapons in the hands of opponents and terrorists – although the North Korean aims its tough talk at the US.

4. **Allies:** The US has strong defense allies around the world – NATO (all of the nations of western Europe and some now of Eastern Europe), Australia, New Zealand, Japan, and South Korea. Defense cooperation agreements or understandings are there with several other nations – India, Egypt, Pakistan, South-east Asian nations (SEATO), etc.

5. **Terrorism:** This is NOT an existentialist threat – it does not threaten the existence of the United States. It does not threaten the existence of the United States- but it needs to be managed better. The main battle against terrorism is not on the battle field, but in the hearts and minds of the people worldwide – we have to have better alternatives, and convince people (especially the young) that we have a better ideology. The US is not waging a good ideological war, and neither has the approach or rhetoric that can help it take the moral high ground to convince the minds of the young from getting radicalized – the radical groups portray the US and western civilization as commercially and socially immoral. The less this is portrayed as a religious war, the better. Unfortunately, Trump is making this much worse with his sectarian talk.

The US has a very well-funded defense establishment – as per Wikipedia, Under Obama, the base US Defense budget grew from about $ 530 billion in 2010 to about $ 553 billion in 2012, before declining slightly to $534 billion in 2016. **The US has nine commands that cover every area of the world – these are the Northern, Southern, Central, European, Pacific, Africa, Strategic, Special Operations and Transportation Commands.** It is the only nation that can project power all over the world, and has bases, troops and facilities located at suitable points so it can provide an adequate response anywhere it needs to.

With Trump, with the recent budget deal to keep the government open, there has been a vast increase in the Defense budget from about $ 583 billion for Fiscal Year (FY) 2017, to about $ 700 billion for FY 2018, and further increased to $ 716 billion for FY 2019. This represents about a 23% increase in just two years. Considering the big tax cut that Trump got passed, this will add massively to the US Federal Deficit. Even experts are saying that this massive increase in defense spending is unnecessary and that the massive increases in the federal deficit will endanger the nation more. Earlier, following 9/11, George W. Bush increased defense spending from $432 billion to $ 789 billion, or an 83% increase while cutting taxes, which began to lead to massive increases in the federal deficit. This level of defense spending is unsustainable and will ultimately weaken the nation. The military budget actually remained quite steady under Obama, and contrary to what Trump is saying, Obama actually initiated many new big military developments like a new bomber, ballistic missile submarine, cruise missile, and intercontinental ballistic missile (ICBM).

The 2004 Defense Posture review under Bush tried to change the whole strategy of US Defense from the Cold War era of fighting organized national militaries, and that of technological superiority only, to that of flexibility in its response and capabilities. The five themes that came out of this review that were used to upgrade capabilities were: Improve flexibility and contend with uncertainty, strengthen allied roles and build new partnerships, create the capacity to act both within and across regions, develop rapidly deployable capabilities, and focus of effective military capabilities –

not numbers of units, personnel or equipment. The 2011 review under Obama took a historical look at how the US military had operated and further updated its defense posture so as to be able to flexibly meet the challenges under the future. With a high level of spending and a flexible upgrade of its capabilities, the US today dominates the land, air, sea and space.

Trumps wild and strongman type talk and bravado has done little to strengthen the US or make the world a more peaceful place, or one that suits or is to the liking of the rich and powerful of the US. Meanwhile it has weakened our defense posture as even our allies do not know if the US can be relied on. His rhetoric on North Korea has made the peninsula a much more dangerous place and increased their activity and tough talk – with an increased pace of both missile and nuclear development.

Hitler and his axis allies prevailed and dominated the field in World War II for a while. It is fortunate that the US was there to build up and combining with the colonial partners of the British (like the British Indian army troops), and the Australian ally in the Pacific, and cooperating with the Soviet Union that defeated Germany in the east, was able to eventually defeat Germany, Italy and Japan. **The most dangerous situation that the world faces today is that Trump is in command of the most powerful military of the world.** Should he begin to behave irresponsibly, there are few nations out there who could stand up to the US in the short term. Both for good of the US and the world, Trump and his political allies need to be politically overcome.

So the vision for defense is the opposite of what Trump is doing and more in line with the nation's and the world's real defense needs: (1) Reduce defense spending down to a more sustainable level so as to not contribute to big federal deficits, (2) Strengthen US cooperation with our allies around the globe and have strengthened defense cooperation with regimes that are democratic, (3) Rather than the US being the sole policeman of the world, build a multi-lateral arrangement for keeping the peace in the world, in cooperation with our allies – with a strengthened peace keeping role for the United Nations, and some mechanisms for resolving differences with other powers (4) The US should continue to maintain an ability to project power globally, but cooperate with our allies to step up and pay a greater role in their own areas, (5) The terrorist threat requires a more ideological approach, where we have to able to convince people in the countries dominated by terrorism that what we have to offer by the way of progress is financially, morally and socially superior, but accommodates different ideas form those countries, as long as the process is democratic, and (6) Get back to a nuclear non-proliferation process that convinces and involves all nations that currently have nuclear weapons to begin to reduce nuclear weapons, and to persuade others not to get them. The US must get back in a stronger way to being a broker of peace around the world, and lead by example, while making sure that those who create trouble, and/or conflict situations are dealt with firmly, so as to ensure that the humanitarian and basic needs of all people are well looked after.

Healthcare for All – Making America Healthy

In 2015 the US spent $3.2 trillion on healthcare, which was 17.8% of the Gross Domestic product (GDP). At the same time overall, the inactivity levels of Americans are high, nutrition is still poor and obesity levels remain high. Health statistics in terms of infant mortality remain poorest among most developed nations. The Affordable Care Act (Obamacare) was an attempt to try and improve the healthcare for many Americans that did not have good healthcare coverage. Trump and he Republicans are trying to pull even this modest attempt, and Trumpcare is much worse than Obamacare.

The US already shows a very low level of health compared to other developed nations, in spite of being the richest nation in terms of per capita income (total income divided by population). As of 2017, the US ranks 37th out of 191 nations in overall healthcare performance. United States has life expectancy of 78.8 years, much lower than Japan's at 83.9 years; infant mortality of 5,8 per 1,000 live births (versus Japan's 2.0; healthcare spending per capita (average) of $ 10,348; and on top of that 44% of the population does not go to a doctor when sick or injured, 40% skip tests or treatments, 40% fearing the bill more than the illness, and 30% having to choose between medical bills and basic necessities.

The aspects of healthcare that we need to look at are – the health of the population without considerations of medical care, the cost and quality of healthcare, the availability and affordability of healthcare to all people, and the need to invest in good health as a competitive national issue. On the health of the population before medical care, while it is true that the US does very well in Olympics competition, the general health of the population requires much to be desired and requires a high level of medical care.

The Vision that appears to be the best for America is Universal Healthcare or a single payer healthcare system. As an example, California's total healthcare costs would go from $ 368 billion down to $ 331 billion, plus everyone would be covered with a high level of preventative and curative healthcare. Also, this would mean a total elimination of the high levels of underinsured and uninsured people, most of whom spend too much on healthcare relative to their incomes. The Single Payer system would cover all healthcare needs, end public fear and insecurity, stop bureaucratic interference with treatments, create a single medical data system to establish accountability, eliminate medical bankruptcies, end all out of pocket costs, provide relief to businesses and farmers, and help doctors focus on taking care of the health of their patients, rather than spending so much time on responding to insurance companies, reduce the cost of drugs as the single payer system could get the drug companies to competitively bid for business. Imagine a healthcare system that is better, covers everybody, and saves the average citizen a lot of money by savings on direct payments, and on drugs. The opponents are the insurance companies, drug companies, right wing Republicans and their super PACs like the Koch brothers. It's time to overcome them and deliver what the American people really need.

Investing in Our People – Making America Competitive – Better Education

There is no doubt that the true wealth of a nation is the quality of its people, meaning their health, education, skills, civic participation and productivity. After World War II, the nations that recovered the fastest, even though they were totally destroyed and had few natural resources, were nations where the people were educated, skilled, healthy and creative! The examples are Germany and Japan – it's true that the US helped them, but other nations that the US helped did not do as well. Unfortunately for many decades now, the US has neglected education. While many of the private colleges and universities are world class and attract students from all over the world, the US education system is woefully inadequate. This big deficiency has been made up in the past 70 years by an immigration policy that enabled the migration of highly educated and skilled people in the deficiency areas from other nations. At the same time, US students suffer from crushing levels of student debt, especially for those attending ivy league schools.

The nation needs adequate funding for free or heavily subsidized education in all public schools, community colleges, and universities, so that all students who meet certain minimum academic standards can get a basic education. This will greatly increase the quality of the output from our schools and colleges. For private schools and colleges, there need to be strong financing at affordable terms of student loans.

Reforming Trade and Wall Street to Create Prosperity for Main Street

After World War II, after having suffered through trade protectionism and wall street excesses that led to the Great Depression, the nations of the world, led by the US, established the **General Agreement on Tariffs and Trade (GATT)**. First signed by 23 nations on October 30, 1947, it went into force on January 1, 1948, GATT was a legal agreement aimed at reducing or eliminating trade barriers like tariffs and quotas. This led to trade liberalization, tariff reductions and an increase in trade between the nations that joined formed and joined GATT. However, from the beginning Trade agreements and negotiations have been conducted in secrecy, without citizen participation and involvement, and have always been written with strong input by large corporations and financial interests, for their own benefit. Because of this, workers' rights, and health and safety concerns have always been sacrificed when arriving at the trade agreements.

The last round of trade negotiations, called the Uruguay Round, led to the formation of the **World Trade Organization (WTO) by 123 nations on April 14, 1994.** It was during the negotiations that led to the formation of the WTO, especially during the 1991-94 period) that the writer became aware of the issues and how WTO came to be formed. **As was in the earlier trade negotiations that led to changes in GATT, the negotiations that led to the formation of WTO, were again dominated by large corporations and financial interests. Non-governmental organizations (NGOs) that represented the broader interests of people for fair working**

conditions, a clean environment, and health and safety considerations were sacrificed. As a clear example, US herbicide and pesticide regulations on imported agricultural food products before WTO were among the tightest in the world, with a clear understanding that this was needed for the good health of all US consumers. However, an organization called Codex Alimentarius in Italy, helped trade negotiators come up with "harmonized" set of rules that lowered these standards and allowed much higher pesticide and herbicide residues on imported food. Standards and regulations that people had fought hard for and established by the US democratic process were over-ruled and replaced by WTO rules that were more favorable to Agri-Business.

The North America Free Trade Agreement (NAFTA), initiated by George H.W. Bush, was signed into law on January 1, 1994 by president Bill Clinton. This established a free trade agreement between Canada, the US and Mexico. The advantages (pros) of NAFTA were that it greatly increased trade, provided some increase in economic output (0.5% for the US), is supposed to have provided job growth (overall – but led to the loss of manufacturing jobs – see below), increased foreign direct investment in each other's nations, lowered prices for oil imports from Mexico, and helped government spending (supposedly because companies in any nation could bid on government contracts in all nations. The disadvantages (cons) were that the US lost as many as 750,000 manufacturing jobs (most moving to Mexico, where labor was cheap), it suppressed wages (this was used by companies to weaken unions), cheaper US farm exports put as many as 1.3 million Mexican farmers out of work and increased their migration to the US, Mexican farmers went to work in substandard working conditions in the Maquiladoras (industries along the border), increased pollution in Mexico as Agri-business was forced to use more fertilizers an herbicides and pesticides to try and compete, and marginal farmers cut down forests in effort to survive, and lower safety Mexican trucks were allowed to enter the US. Ross Perot, a former presidential candidate had been right during his campaign that NAFTA would mean a giant sucking sound of manufacturing jobs going down to Mexico, and he was right, but neither of the two major parties had agreed with him.

The Trans Pacific Partnership (TPP) between the US and 11 other Pacific Rim nations, was intended by the United States to reduce China's influence, and reduce trade of those eleven nations with China. Withdrawing from TPP, Trump is actually helping China gain an advantage, the opposite of what he is trying to do – although, since it would hurt the working class, that part of his base would like it. Since Trump has withdrawn the US from the trade deal, the other nations have gone ahead with what they have called the Comprehensive and Progressive Agreement for TPP. As with other trade agreements (which have been generally dominated by the United States), the benefits in terms of trade, investment, intellectual property, and profits generally would go to the large corporations and financial businesses, while hurting the interests of workers, unions, and the environment, and the interests of public and worker health and safety.

Looking at the bigger financial system, there are many big aspects that impact the well-being of the nation, and especially the common people. These are the areas of trade and financial regulation. Contrary to what Trump has been saying, trade agreements that the US has arrived at have actually been influenced by and been good for big US companies and financial institutions. The US has won big concessions from other nations, especially the poor nations that have helped big companies to do what they want, move production facilities where they want, avoid environmental costs and regulations in the US, by moving production to other nations that enable production facilities that pollute those nations, engage in sweatshop labor, and have unsafe working conditions (which the big collapse of a Bangladesh garment factory revealed). Trade policy and trade agreements have helped the big companies to make hefty profits, but have been bad for US workers, and bad for the environment of other nations and the world.

So, Trade agreements need to be reformed, not by engaging in trade wars like Trump is doing, which will lead to a global recession (like it contributed to the great depression). The trade agreements need to be renegotiated and reformed so as to be better for US workers, not allow sweatshop conditions for foreign labor, not allow companies to escape environmental regulations by polluting other nations or exporting toxic waste, and not allow all production to be moved overseas by insisting on certain minimum levels of Made in America provisions (which by the way Obama had already done!).

Protecting Our Financial System & Our Economy

After global warming, one of the biggest dangers facing the US and the world is the threat of another Financial Crisis like the one in 2008, which was rescued from being a big Depression by Obama and the Federal Reserve Bank. The financial crisis was caused by George W. Bush and the Republicans in deregulating the financial sector and not policing them when they began to steal from the economy through risky behavior. The horrors that surfaced were huge, and people came to know of extremely complicated transactions like Credit Default Swaps and many others like that which had been used by the financial robber barons to engage in their irresponsible behavior. These financial institutions and their leaders should have been the ones to pay a price and bene punished for their misdeeds, and instead the common people paid a very heavy price. In the month that Obama took office, the US was losing 800,000 jobs per month! Millions lost their jobs, their homes and their well-being, and the slow recovery that Obama was able to manage got the US back from the brink and, together with the Federal Reserve Bank was able to help the US economy to recover. The European Union and its nations did not engage in putting money into their economies in the same way, causing a bigger crisis there and big problems for Greece and Spain.

With Trump in power, and with deregulations and a similar lack of policing of the financial companies, the same danger has surfaced, for the US and the world. The Great Depression of the 1930s resulted from stock market speculation, deregulation of companies, trade wars leading to big time protectionism by nations, a president and congress that did not believe in governments rescuing the economy, and the lack of the insurance of bank checking and savings deposits. **So, for the US economy, this is the biggest danger is another Great Depression,** triggered by the actions of Trump – deregulation of the financial companies, trade wars, tax cuts (meaning government is not out there spending money – so less buying going on out there), less policing of financial bad actors, decreasing safety nets and pensions, and healthcare coverage (meaning people have less money to spend – bad for business!).

THE REJUVENATE GUIDE

STRATEGIES FOR IMPLEMENTING THE VISION

This book and the accompanying manual have been written in order to energize and facilitate fresh visions of what the United States of America can be like, to unify and energize the movements that have come up in opposition to Trump and the Republicans, and provide enough material for health and beneficial alternatives, so that the candidates that we help win elections have some real mandates to improve the nation, make it better for the middle class and poor who have suffered so much with the predatory actions of Republicans and the robber barons they have encouraged. The big companies must earn their way by doing things that are truly beneficial, innovative, and create jobs and opportunities, while providing real value in terms of products and services.

This book and the accompanying manual are a real call for the nation to pick up the threads, overcome the negative and replace it politically, economically and environmentally with a movement, emphasis and approach that leads the nation in a direction that Americans can be proud of and which brings together people of all races, religions, national origins, genders and sexual orientations.

A DETAILED LIST OF ACTION ITEMS

This is a starting Guide for all those seeking to reverse the Trump agenda and replace it with a vision of our own – the rest of America. Each of us needs to be armed with these action items and be ready to push candidates in upcoming elections to ask questions and demand responsiveness to issues that are good for all the common people of this nation. Between elections, adopt the Indivisible Guide action items. Revise and add to the guide and propose revisions or additions to the Vision for your own use.

Get to Work Making it Happen!

Overall
- Demand that candidates make commitments not to accept money from corporate interests, the NRA, and fossil fuel companies. Ask candidates about their sources of funding.
- While working hard on the issue that is most important to you, support all of the major movements and organizations described above
- Remember that for defeating the Republican Candidates, and getting your favorite opposition candidate elected, you will find that all the other movements are your allies

Political Strategies for Resisting Interference in Elections
- Recommend all Candidates, especially crucial ones that they harden their computer systems against hacking – donate to the ones that are vulnerable
- Recommend that all unfavorable advertisements on social media and traditional media be questioned in to determine who the persons are that are funding the ads. If foreign nationals, it be demanded that these by pulled right away.
- Refuse to give personal data to social media, unless one is sure that the location is safe and secure location of one's own party and organization, and info will be secure.
- Rapidly respond to all false (Fake) news that are generated and circulated and make sure that the news is rapidly neutralized

Political Strategies for Resisting Opposition Political Strategies
- Political advertisements taken out by Republican PACs be immediately called out for false or damaging reporting with counter narratives and strategy adopted to neutralize
- Develop and fund consistent advertisements that promote the narratives of our alternative positions and visions, and why these are better for America

- MANY important Republicans are voicing their absolute rejection of Trump and how they hate his policies, actions and language – They are urging voters not to vote Republican! Encourage such people and amplify their news and message to other Republicans and to all of our supporters

Some Items Based on Indivisible Guide Action Items Summary (Here for your convenience)

- Have strong grassroots advocacy – target local members of the congress and senate
  - If Republican legislators and candidates – oppose and criticize
  - If Democratic or Independent – support but demand responsiveness to our demands for reform of the Democratic party (Use Vision section as a guide)
- Adopt a Defensive Approach focused on stopping Trump from implementing agenda based on racism, authoritarianism and corruption
- Identify, Organize and Mobilize your Local Group – cooperate to make things happen
- Reach out to all voters, young and old, especially those that might be staying away till now – register, motivate and energize them – USE this manual to motivate them!
- Local Advocacy actions that work
  - Show up at Town Hall meetings – if Republican let them know your views on issues important to you
  - If Democrat, make sure that you say you support them in the upcoming election, but convince them to be stronger on issues important to you

Canvassing Activity

- Now, before the election it is very important that you help the maximum with the following activities
  - Help with phone banks for crucial Democratic candidates, especially ones that will help us take the House and the Senate back

o Do door to door canvassing for candidates, issues and your local group – provide guidance to voters on how to vote on candidates and ballot measures – this overcomes their hesitation to get out and vote

Action Items Based on the Section on Detailed Vision Above

NOTE: The importance of this section is to make you aware of all the list of issues and action items. It is most probable that you may be better at defining the Action Items for the issue that is most important to you. However, the aim here is to make you aware that the action items in other issue areas need your support, because you will find that you are opposing the same candidates – hence by joining forces you will be stronger and more effective!

Strengthening Our Democracy Action Items

- **Overall:** Because of Trump's attack on all aspects of our Democracy, getting him out of power has to be a top priority. Along with him, and supporters of him must never get elected, and his supreme court nominee must not be approved. Next, any Tea Party republicans must be soundly defeated, as they are the ones responsible for grid lock – they obstructed Obama all the way. Tea Partiers in the House did not allow Immigration reforms to become law in 2006 and 2013, even though the Senate on both occasions sent them bills with more than 60% of the Senators approving. Next, Republicans that oppose Democratic Party and Progressive proposals for improving the country must also be soundly defeated.
- President Lyndon B. Johnson signed into law the Voting Rights Act of 1965 that was intended to overcome legal barriers that prevented African Americans from voting as guaranteed by the 15th amendment to the constitution. But

Republicans continue to use every method possible to create obstacles in the path of minority voters. All efforts to suppress voting, such as voter IDs, restricted hours, and purging voter rolls at state or national levels need to be fought. All efforts to suppress voting, such as voter IDs, restricted hours, and purging voter rolls at state or national levels need to be fought

- Currently prisoners and those who have served their time are not allowed to vote. This discriminates mainly against African and Latin Americans. Candidates for election should vow to introduce legislation to restore these rights.

- Call for an amendment to the Voting Rights Act that does the following: Automatically registers voters when they turn 18, eliminates the purging of voter rolls, makes voting day a federal holiday, and empowers people to have a say in early voting, polling locations and dates/times.

- Call for eliminating the politically bad practice of Gerrymandering that has enabled the drawing of district maps in such a way that tries to ensure that Republicans get elected. In this regard support the efforts of the National Democratic Redistricting Committee (NDRC) – so that district boundaries are drawn logically and not to favor Republicans. Although the next national redistricting will occur in 2021, NDRC efforts need support now, in order that we succeed in 2021 (https://democraticredistricting.com/about/)

- Fight to end the buying of our elections by big money, anonymous donors, billionaires, and big lobbying interests. This is most damaging to our democracy. Citizens United ruling by the Supreme Court must be overturned. But candidates for elections should also vow not to take Corporate or NRA money.

- **First Amendment Rights:** We must fight and push back at all attempts to attack and weaken our media and press, attempts to financially control all of the media (like the Sinclair case), and must fight to protect the safety and security of journalists. At the same time, we need to put all media companies and organizations on notice that corporations or any given party should not control or show total bias for one party (as Fox News does)

- **Protecting Our Judiciary & Preventing its Politicization:** We must fight and push back at all attacks on the Judiciary and try at every turn to ensure their impartiality and total adherence to the US Constitution. At the same time, we have to oppose the politicization of the Judiciary: Classic case, we need to oppose the appointment of Brent Cavanaugh to the Supreme Court. Currently the Court has allowed insane amounts of money to influence elections (falsely arguing this on the basis of free speech, and allowing corporations to be considered as persons), and weakened labor rights and hence those of all working people.

- It's Time to END the Electoral College Method of Choosing a President. It allowed Donald Trump to become president even though Hillary Clinton won the popular vote by about 2.8 million votes. Why should one states vote count more than another's? Even if the elector system remains, states need to support the National Popular Vote Interstate Compact, that if enough states sign up, will direct all elector votes to be automatically cast for the popular vote winner.

The Democratic Party Needs Internal Reforms

- A major issue of the Democratic Party is the need for greater internal democracy, and making it more participatory and transparent. Newcomers and others wanting to have their voices and issues heard, often feel discouraged, and this may be a reason many don't join and often don't vote. You need to add your voice to the need for change – this has been defined by the Report of the Unity Reforms Commission (for more details see the book).

- This Report outlines the following four areas that need reform

- o Argue for reform in the manner of voting during the presidential nominating process, and recommend measures that increase participation and inclusion.
- o The second is to make the caucuses encourage participation and inclusion.
- o The third area is to eliminate unpledged delegates that appear to favor one candidate over another. As an organization, while requiring that all candidates adhere to the values of the party and all its allies, the party should not favor one candidate over the other.
- o The fourth area is the party reforms that make our candidates more competitive in every region, broadening the party's base, empowering democrats at the local level, and expanding the party's donor base
- Anyone who has been recently energized or wants to jump in and help, should find a readiness and an openness to be accepted, not only in the presidential nomination process, but also in all issues of concern.
- So, at every Party gathering, ask for and emphasize the need for these reforms, and if not already implemented, push for them to get implemented

The Democratic Party Needs to Learn from Failures & Expand its Tent

- The 2016 election and even the last decade have seen a massive reversal in the fortunes of the party. Even though earlier it saw Obama got elected, and held a majority in the Congress and Senate for two years, the party has not only lost that control since then, but has lost about a thousand legislative seats as the state level, and there are only 6-7 states where the party has dominance in terms of governorships and majority in state legislatures. You should press for the Democratic Party to learn from its mistakes and reform its structure, its base and its extent.

- There have been many marches and movements, such as the Women's March, Climate March, Gun Control March, Criminal Justice Related marches, and Immigration marches. There is also now a Progressive movement such as Our Revolution and Progressive Democrats of America. The Democratic Party, in order to succeed needs to bring all of these movements under its tent, or at least form a coalition with these movements with clearly drawn up rules and action plans for cooperation. You should be pressing the Democratic Party to do this.

- The Progressive wing of the democratic party provided an analysis of what produced the failures, and produced a report that included recommendations on how to revitalize the party. This report is titled, "Autopsy: A Democratic Party in Crisis". For a more detailed description please read the book or the report itself.

- Overall, the report states that, "During the 2016 general election, the party experienced a falloff of voter turnout and support among people of color, the young and the working class." Much of our report concentrates on assessing the Democratic Party's approach to those demographic groups. It faults the continuing chase after elusive republican voters and neglecting or ignoring its base.

- The Report Stated that: One of the large groups with a voter-turnout issue is young people, "who encounter a toxic combination of a depressed economic reality, GOP efforts at voter suppression, and anemic messaging on the part of Democrats."

- "Emerging sectors of the electorate are compelling the Democratic Party to come to terms with adamant grassroots rejection of economic injustice, institutionalized racism, gender inequality, environmental destruction and corporate domination. Siding with the people who constitute the base isn't truly possible when party leaders seem to be afraid of them."

- Democratic Party candidates (as Clinton did) and legislators need to stop being Hawkish about issues of war, taking that as a symbol of nationalism – the insane increases in the Defense Budget need to be controlled (see section on US Defense below). Supporting our Troops is not the same as wasting money and taking a war like approach to everything.
- As this manual and accompanying Book urge: "This is about more than just increasing voter turnout. It is about energizing as well as expanding the base of the party. To do this we must aggressively pursue two tracks: fighting right-wing efforts to rig the political system, and giving people who can vote a truly compelling reason to do so."
- "The enduring point of community outreach is to build an ongoing relationship that aims for the party to become part of the fabric of everyday life. It means acknowledging the validity and power of people-driven movements as well as recognizing and supporting authentic progressive community leaders. It means focusing on how the party can best serve communities, not the other way around. Most of all, it means persisting with such engagement on an ongoing basis, not just at election time."
- As described below in this manual, in its programs and policies, the Democratic Party needs to pay attention to issues such as healthcare for all, economic issues that benefit the working class, the true equality of all women, criminal justice reform that benefits people of color and end its neglect of rural citizens and farm families. At the same time, the Democratic party needs to "disentangle itself -- ideologically and financially -- from Wall Street, the military-industrial complex and other corporate interests that put profits ahead of public needs"
- **One of the things that this manual and the accompanying book proposes, that is different,** is that the Democratic Party, rather than staying away from core economy issues relating to Economy, financial interests, corporate interests, and the military industrial complex, should propose and

implement reforms of these massive areas of the economy and national life, so that they serve the genuine interests of Americans at all levels (rather than only those who are rich), and propose policies, programs and strategies that are good for America and good for the world. Not doing that will always mean like fretting about the horse after it has bolted the barn. These are described in the sections that follow.

Push for Superior Strategies on Jobs & Economy

- There is no doubt that it's the economy that creates and destroys jobs, but that it is the main elephant in the room whose functioning needs to be addressed. But the needs of our people and planet Earth have changed, and if we have to survive and flourish as a species, we need innovation and changes in our economy, in our technologies, in our systems of ownership and control, in how we measure progress, and in how the fruits gets distributed. In the past, innovation has mainly been the means of increasing company profits or transforming the economy by creating winners and losers. Now we need innovation on how we can empower a distributed innovation, innovation to improve the prospects for and productivity of life on the planet (rejuvenate planet Earth), and in transforming our economy to create a system that provides a good healthy life for all.
- Before we go to a better policy to truly creating better paying jobs and manufacturing jobs, it is important to emphasize that a minimum wage of $ 15 is needed across the board so that everyone who works gets paid a living wage – sweatshop underpaid labor is no longer an option. We should stop buying goods and services from companies and retail stores that do not pay their employees a decent minimum wage.
- The Democratic party and all opposing Trump and the Republicans need a much stronger strategy on Jobs & Economy (which Republicans now dominate). Democrats should be supporters of the right kind of Business

approaches, financial investments, industrial policy/strategy and tax reforms.

- We need to advocate Tax reform but one that is pro-employment and pro-environment. For example, businesses should be able to depreciate human capital development (training), and depreciation of capital equipment should be stretched out. There should be tax breaks for hiring more people too. The Trump tax cuts are not providing and incentive to businesses to train or hire more people.

- We need to advocate Industrial Development policy and programs that are pro-employment. Like the promotion of industries that provide greater employment – their development from R&D, to support for product development, financing and marketing (this is how Japan came up and began to dominate many areas of technology, and it is what China is doing RIGHT NOW).

- For Depressed communities, rural areas and small towns, promote local production for local use. The processing of agricultural crops should be promoted. Also, for previous coal towns promote training and investment in solar and wind energy. Internet connectivity, rural electrification, better education, and better healthcare and access to doctors should become high on the Democratic Party list – no reason why the Rural areas continue to be Red (Republican dominated).

- The economy of the future, that solves the climate change problem, needs training and employment in new types of sustainability type activities, for example, energy efficiency (new and retro-fitted buildings), mass transit, bike transportation, sustainable (alternative) agriculture that uses less water fertilizer and bio-cides, and sustainable forestry (that keep forests standing but only extracts small amounts by labor intensive means).

- Trade agreements have been pro-big business and pro-large corporations (It's a company that wants to make bigger profits that moves its manufacturing to another state or another country). Call for renegotiating trade agreements so that they are more pro-employment and pro-environment – force worker compensation, minimum wages (not just in the US, but abroad), outlaw sweatshop labor, mandate environmental and worker safety standards (horror of Bangladesh textile factory disaster due to unsafe conditions), encourage direct trade between small companies, and force companies to relocate laid off workers.

Solutions to Climate Change and the Environmental Crisis

- As soon as the Trump regime is gone, we must emphasize that we have to get back on the Paris Agreement.
- But we have to do more than that – we have to again take up the global leadership to make this happen globally – Remember that Global warming is a GLOBAL problem. **We need the cooperation of ALL of the nations of the world to make it happen.**
- We need to push for the formation and empowerment of a global organization that will actually help the world make this transition to a low carbon world very rapidly. Technologies, techniques, resources, grids, education, training all have to come together, with the US and western nations (and even Japan and China) taking the lead and helping the poorer and less resourceful nations in making the transition.
- There are four aspects that need attention: The rapid reduction in the use of fossil fuels and ones that emit carbon or cause the greenhouse effect, transitioning to clean energy (renewables like solar, wind and geothermal, and energy efficiency)the restoration of global ecosystems (forests, oceans, mountains and deserts) that absorb carbon, and the preparation and implementation of disaster mitigation plans (for preparing and minimizing damage caused by wildfires, hurricanes, coastal storms, tornados, massive floods, etc.)

- We need to restore the EPA beyond where it was in the past, and ensure that the water, air and soil is cleaned, and the health of the population is protected. Companies need to be helped meet environmental regulations, through technical financial and incentive support.
- We have to absolutely refuse to take money and support from fossil fuel companies, as this works against our efforts to solve the climate change crisis. Workers in such companies should be encouraged to donate individually and belong to and support the Democratic party and opposition to Trump and the Republicans, but the Democratic Party must not accept donations and funding from PACs connected with fossil fuel companies. This must parallel the efforts for disinvestment in fossil fuel companies – efforts such as Fossil Free California.

Women's Rights Must be Strengthened Until We Get Equality

- Our strength as a nation and fairness to all individuals requires that women become equal in all ways. Women need to be empowered to be totally equal members of society in every way. You have to push for strengthening of women's rights!
- The Women's March and other marches have proved that women and their supporters are active – it is now important that this activity be turned into political action!
- (The following action items are based on the content from the National Organization for Women (NOW) website, and some text may be the same)
- Reproductive Rights & Justice: Women should have the right to make all decisions about their bodies, as they can affect life and death issues, and the status of their health. This means we must support access to safe and legal abortion, effective birth control and emergency contraception, reproductive health services, and education for all women.

- Economic Justice: Women must have total equality in economic matters including welfare reform, provision for a livable wage, job discrimination, equal pay for equal work, housing, and social security and pension reform. They must also have equality in jobs, housing, business and finance. Special attention needs also to be paid to the needs in this area of the women of color, so as to ensure racial justice as well.
- Ending Violence Against Women: All aspects of the problem of violence must be fully addressed: "domestic violence, sexual assault, sexual harassment, violence at abortion clinics, hate crimes cross lines of gender, sexuality and race, the gender bias in our judicial system, and the violence of poverty" – discrimination against poor women. Candidates for office must agree to stronger and more effective measures at their respective legislatures.
- LGBTQ Rights: As per NOW, we must "fight discrimination based on sexual orientation or gender identity in all areas, including employment, housing, public accommodations, health services, child custody and military policies." Educational efforts must fight homophobia, and promote positive images and ensure their civil rights.
- Constitutional Equality: The US Constitution needs to guarantee equality in pay, job opportunities, political status, social security, and education. The last effort at ratifying the Equal Rights Amendment (ERA, passed by congress in 1972, but ratified only by 35 states, less than the 38 needed) had failed and officially ended in 1982. However, 37 states have ratified it as of this date and if another state ratifies it, then given a favorable Congress in the future, Congress has the power to accept this and hence ratify the ERA. We must push candidates and legislators to push to ratify the ERA!

Reducing Gun Violence

- The Never Again movement has brought this issue to a head, but for many years now, people have been active in trying to stop the gun violence that plagues America.
- We have to push for the defeat of candidates who accept money from the NRA, those in the Republican party that accept money from them or stand in the way of gun control. Democratic candidates who do not begin to support strong legislation and action must be discouraged.
- Push for the strengthening of background checks, and disallow all categories that can be prone to gun violence – felons, fugitives and domestic abusers – those suffering from mental health, have criminal records, court martialed military, are on the terrorist watch list, etc. The Brady Law that was signed on February 28, 1994 started the process, now let's finish it.
- Push for the responsibility of gun owners to keep their guns safe from other family members, and when a person passes away, their guns should be turned into police department. Gun owners must be held accountable for their guns.
- Bump stocks and assault weapons must be banned. A Bump stock replaces the standard rifle stock so as to allow the stock to slide back and forth between shoulder and trigger finger, that enables a rifle to fire rounds almost as rapidly as a machine gun. Assault rifles are rifles designed to fire rapidly in a semi-automatic or fully automatic mode. Both types are capable of killing large numbers of people in a very short time. That gun owners need to protect themselves from a tyrannical government is a laughable argument – the US military can defeat ALL foreign armies as of today – so civilian resisters can be no match.
- Concealed Carry laws must be curtailed, that allow people to carry weapons everywhere without others knowing that they are carrying them. Open carry or concealed carry are ways of threatening others, rather than just for self-protection.

- We have to begin supporting more funding and support for mental healthcare programs, so that those suffering from mental issues are truly taken care of and do not need to be running around untended on the streets or displaying their anger through the use of guns (see healthcare section below)

Healthcare for All

- The following is based on the description in the Our Revolution Website, and from the Healthcare for All – California website. Some emphasis and arguments have been added.
- Added reasons - A healthy nation is a strong, productive, generous and happy nation! Healthcare for all is an important investment for America!
- As a minimum, we must totally restore all provisions of the Affordable Care Act (Obamacare) and work to strengthen it by correcting any deficiencies. Trumpcare, which is what Trump is seeking to replace it with is totally anti-people and would cause large numbers of people to be without health insurance, and people would again be refused insurance because of pre-existing conditions.
- We must demand a federally administered Single Payer Healthcare system that provides comprehensive healthcare for all Americans. This will provide coverage for all health needs, and enable patients to access the provider of their choice. This also goes by the name of Medicare for all, and is NOT Socialist, but a capitalist system but with only one customer (Medicare), who buys health services and drugs from all private sector providers.
- A Federal Single Payer system will lower the healthcare costs for the nation, which are more than double that of most other developed nations, lower drug costs by enabling the system to negotiate prices, and make the USA more competitive than other nations, as the cost of doing business will go down. Drug and insurance companies will need to adjust and accept a reasonable profit, instead of the

huge profits they have enjoyed. A system of incentives can be worked out, where in cooperation with the National Institutes of Health, drug makers can earn a reasonable profit for developing new drugs without charging insane prices!

- When questioned, provide the example of Senate Bill SB 562 introduced in California for a Single Payer system of healthcare, which will stabilize costs, cut waste, free patients and doctors to make healthcare decisions, maintain an excellent health care delivery network, and make the "best health care in the world" available to all in America. Patients would receive comprehensive benefits and suitable care.

Action for Sensible Immigration Reform

- Before the coming of Trump, most of the American people, the presidents and the Senators have been pushing for Immigration Reform. In 2006, under George Bush and under Obama in 2013, the Senate passed Immigration Reform Bills and sent them to the House for consideration, and both presidents were willing to sign them. With arrogance, on both occasions, the House refused even to consider the bills. In 2013, the trouble makers were Tea Party Republicans, who, together with Trump supporters must be voted out of office for the nation to move forward.
- The Native Americans immigrated to North America thousands of years ago – they say, during the last ice age, when Asia and America were connected by an ice bridge in the region of Alaska. Everyone else who came to America immigrated without legal permission from current inhabitants. Even after independence, many waves of immigrants came, mainly from Europe, but also from all other parts of the world. The USA is a land of immigrants.
- The Trump administration, through ICE and other means has introduced and atmosphere of fear for undocumented people, and legal permanent residents and even citizens

from non-European countries. Also, at the border, they have separated children from parents from those crossing and seeking asylum. These policies should be fully criticized and abolished, and all children should be united with their parents.

- Because there is much confusion about immigration, it is best to lay out the best available Immigration Reform plan that had received a broad measure of bi-partisan support, except from Tea Party Republican extremists.

- The following action points are based on the **2013 Immigration reform bill that was passed by the US Senate in 2013 by 62 senators voting for it** – these should be used as talking points in proposing what should be done – candidates and activists can use these

- **Border security** to be beefed up by the addition of patrol agents, added fencing and added surveillance technologies. This would be designed to achieve a 100% coverage and to ensure that at least 90% of the would-be crossers are caught and/or turned back. **This would do much better than Trump's so-called Wall.**

- **Undocumented Immigrants:** The approximately 11 million people living in the US illegally would receive "registered provisional immigrant status" providing they arrived in the US before December 31, 2011, have no felony convictions and pay a $500 fine. This would include all young people under DACA status. People in this category could travel and work within the US, would not be eligible for federal benefits, parents deported whose children are citizens or permanent residents would be allowed back, **and this status would continue for 10 years after which they would be eligible to apply for green card status.** Sponsors of those who overstayed their visitor visa period and stayed illegally would be held financially accountable and subject to fines, and required to help locate those who abused this.

- **Temporary Visas for Skilled Workers:** "The cap on the H-1B visa program for high-skilled workers would be raised from

65,000 a year to 110,000 a year, with 25,000 more set aside for people with advanced degrees in science, technology, engineering or math from a U.S. school. The cap could go as high as 180,000 a year depending on demand." Companies that abuse this would be cracked down on.

- Immigrants with **high skill levels** such as professors, researchers, multinational executives and athletes would be exempted from green card limits, as well as graduates with advanced degrees in technology, science, engineering or math.

- A **merit-based visa program** would provide about 250,000 people with visas based on a point system that considers skills, experienced employment, education and period spent in the country. Those with the most points would be eligible.

- The Diversity Visa lottery program that enables 55,000 people from countries that have low levels of immigration to the US should be terminated.

- **Low Skilled Workers**: A new category of visas should allow 200,000 people a year in construction, hospitality, long-term care and other industries. A new agricultural visa program should be established to replace the existing program and be required to go back to their home countries for certain periods of time. People who have already been here for more than a certain period of time would be allowed to remain and work.

- **Family Reunification**: Citizens would be barred from sponsoring their siblings and could only sponsor unmarried children under 31 years of age. Citizens and permanent residents can sponsor their spouses, but the numbers will be kept small. Let's remind Trump that his wife Melania came under this category, and that she in turn sponsored her parents to come to this country.

- **Employment Verification**: Within a certain number of years, all employers must implement E-Verify and verify the legal work status of a non-citizen. All non-citizens would be required to show a photo ID that must match their photo on the E-Verify system.

Strengthening the Fabric of Our Nation - Our Diversity

- **United we stand – divided we fall!** This must be a motto of all Americans. But the activities of those who seek to divide us have to be discouraged. Also, it has to be realized that for the strength of our nation we have to have the loyalty of all citizens and be loyal to all citizens. People of all communities, races, colors, religions, genders, national origins, rural or urban, and sexual orientations MUST be treated and feel like first class citizens. That means that all people must be treated equally and with respect.

- **The fabric of our Diversity contributes to the strength of our nation** and the vibrancy of our democracy. At all times in history, those nations that have celebrated and strengthened their respect for diversity have prospered and those that have not have come to grief.

- **Diversity Education:** We must promote more knowledge and understanding of other cultures, religions, races, genders and sexual orientations. The bigotry, prejudice and hatred that is out there needs to be replaced with understanding, appreciation and respect. No one is superior to another – we have to understand, be respectful, be appreciative and work with people of all types, for our nation to be strong! However, the common democratic and human values described above in the section on the core values that this nation needs – must not be compromised!

- **Rule of Law:** It is important for all people to realize that no matter how high or low they are in power and wealth, or no matter what race or religion they may be, they have to obey the law. It would be well for the president of the United States to remember this! If people think a law is unjust, as per the first amendment rights, they have the right to peacefully protest in the streets without being subjected to police force. Unjust laws that lead to excessive punishment and imprisonment without rehabilitation, have to go and be replaced with laws that favor rehabilitation. The violence being done to communities of color have to end.

- **Injustice against People of Color:** When the most accomplished of black athletes protest at NFL games, they are not being unpatriotic – they are protesting a profoundly disturbing situation that they and their black community members face on the streets, and in the courts and prisons. The nation needs to pay attention! They are crying for help!
- The following are action items that have been proposed that should be considered
- **Criminal Justice Reform No. 1:** We need to proceed on two fronts simultaneously. On one front, police/courts/prison system need to be provided diversity training and get the training so that better police and community relations are achieved in ALL communities, and police are trained so as to not use excessive force and are no allowed to shoot a unless they are being shot at. On the other front community members have to be trained to work with police, obey the rule of law, and be respectful when approached by a police officer. At the same time, there have to be programs and funding for activities that provide meaningful education, training and activities to gainfully employ young folks so that they do not get into a life of crime – they MUST have good options (see the section on Jobs and Economy, relating to uplifting depressed communities of all colors – white, black, blown and yellow).
- **Criminal Justice Reform No. 2:** The laws, the judiciary and the prosecution and defense system have to be reformed so as to minimize detention and only use it as a last resort, eliminate bail requirements, and direct the prison system to help non-violent offenders from getting worse. The emphasis of the court system has to shift from punishment and imprisonment (after safety from violent offenders and sexual predators has been assured), to seeing how the

person can be rehabilitated. The 2.2 million in prison and 7 million being monitored have to be reduced by a shift in priorities. Being tough on crime is good, but being tough on prisoners is not acceptable – they must be rehabilitated.

- **Criminal Justice Reform No. 3:** Today, persons going into prison for minor offenses come out of the system as hardened criminals likely to be violent – this is an insane system and the mental health of those imposing it have to be checked! The entire prison system needs to be reformed so that while the person is doing time, every effort and program is put in place for education, training and job placement so that the person does not get back to a life of crime on being released. The health, education and proper treatment have to be such that. The funding has to shift, prison sizes have to be drastically reduced over time, and the funding has to shift from detention and control to rehabilitation. Scandinavian countries shave done this very well – now it's the turn for the US system to try and achieve some sanity, purpose and health. We have to stop wasting precious tax payer dollars on imprisonment – we have to stop being a police state!

- **Fighting Drugs and Opiates:** The total emphasis on reducing drugs has to shift from fighting drug dealers to fighting drug addiction, rehabilitation of drug users, education and reducing the demand for drugs. Legalization of low level drugs like Marijuana and their non-criminalization should help reduce drugs related crimes. Young men should be provided employment alternatives to pushing drugs.

- **Combatting hate and extremism:** There are more than 900 hate groups around the country according to the Southern Poverty Law Center (SPLC). These groups have to be monitored to make sure they do not break the laws and to try and steer them away from a life of hatred and bigotry. The encouragement being given to these groups by Trump and the white supremacists has to stop! There needs to be education at all levels in schools and communities, and hate groups have to be called out as being bad and destructive to the nation – without any qualifications!

Trade Agreements & Reform

- Trade agreements have been great for large corporations and financial companies and have generally hurt the interests of the working class, the environment and health and safety of the public and the workers. However, Tariffs and trade wars like Trump is engaging in are not the right way to try and solve the problem – and anyway, the main beneficiaries will still be the big companies, while hurting US Farmers, workers and consumers. The number of jobs created due to Trump's tariff actions have yet to be seen.

- There are four reforms of Trade agreements that we should be advancing, none of which are being advocated by the Democratic Party but would greatly enhance the kinds of benefits that the Progressive wing of the party is fighting for. These four reforms are:

- **The Trade Negotiation Process Must Be Democratic:** It must be open, transparent and participatory, enabling both congress and the public to participate through public hearings and comment on proposed rules.

- Protect the rights of labor, their right to unionize and their right to fair and minimum wages. Public and worker health and safety should be primary concerns, and should not be superseded by other concerns.

- Companies should not be able to move from state to state and from nation to nation in order to pay lower wages, avoid paying taxes, avoid environmental regulations, should be held accountable to their community responsibilities in the communities where they operate, buy and sell. Corporations should not be able to settle their disputes in investor to state dispute settlement that undermine democratic power and public interest.

- Farmers must be protected from price fluctuations caused by imports or exports, or tariffs, that hurt their business.

Farmers in other nations must be protected or compensated as well.
- Currency rules, rules of origin, infrastructure investment, and manufacturing policy, in the case of NAFTA, should lead to a level playing field that creates jobs and wage growth in all three nations.
- There should be strong environmental and safety rules that are swiftly enforceable, for trading in timber, wildlife, fisheries, gaining an unfair advantage by polluting locally, and safety of trucks entering your borders.

Financial System Reform & Control
- After Global warming and nuclear war, the biggest danger facing the US and the global community is the risk of a full-scale Depression caused by irresponsible financial behavior by large companies, like the one that led to the 2008 financial crisis. The US economy and financial system is still not protected from a repeat of 2008.
- The companies that caused that were bailed out, and the people, working class and ordinary citizens paid the price for bad robber baron type behavior by the big companies.
- Strict reform and regulation of the financial system is needed so that they do not engage in the kind of risky financial behavior that led to the 2008 financial crisis. Companies need to set up their internal rules and reward systems so that they do not encourage and certainly punish risky financial behaviors by their employees.
- Nationally and globally a strong policing mechanism is needed so that companies do not engage in risky, irresponsible and illegal behavior. There must be institutions and enforcement mechanisms that lead to swift national and global action (like happens in Interpol), to stop bad behavior and take corrective and punitive actions.
- Company mergers should not be allowed that enable financial companies to become bigger than a certain size, and larger companies should be broken up, so that the

failure of one company does not endanger the whole financial system. Companies should be required to carry financial disaster insurance, and governments should not bail out companies that engage in irresponsible behavior.

Action Items Based on the "Our Revolution" Website – Accompanied with some explanations

- Foreword: Income inequality is a primary economic and financial issue for our time. Trade rules, financial operations, the very operation, behavior and actions of big corporations and even politics have been DESIGNED to increase economic equality. As opposed to "trickle down" economics this may be called the giant "sucking up" effect, where wealth is being sucked up from workers, farmers and consumers, so as to concentrate wealth and assets in the hands of the few.
- For Our Revolution, income equality is a defining issue that needs to be addressed – moral, social, economic and political. Over the last 42 years, the real median income for men has fallen by $ 783, while for women, since 2007, real median income has fallen by $ 1,300. One family has more wealth than 130 million Americans.
- Companies have to fulfil their responsibilities to the nation and its communities and people – the message is clear – you cannot continue to take all, continue to keep shipping jobs to China, hide your profits in the Cayman Islands and other tax havens, not pay your fair share of taxes for all the benefits the nation gives you, while the massive needs of the people of this nation are unmet! Those employees that create the income, deserve a better share, and consumers must start insisting on the fact that what they buy should create local jobs!
- Reverse the Tax cuts and impose a number of estate and wealth related taxes. Impose a financial transactions tax, which is paid every time stocks or financial instruments are bought or sold.

- Increase the federal minimum wage from $ 7.25 to $ 15 an hour by 2020. Every person who works should be guaranteed a wage they can live on when they work full time.
- Invest $ 1 trillion on rebuilding crumbling infrastructure creating 13 million jobs. In this manual we think that new low carbon transportation infrastructure should get a higher priority – mass transit, high speed rail, bike transportation, vehicle electrical charging infrastructure, internet service for rural areas, and integrated transportation systems (all modes linked to one another).
- Invest $ 5.5 billion and create 1 million jobs for disadvantaged youth – youth unemployment is a major problem.
- Enact the Paycheck Fairness Act so that women are paid the same as men for same work – right now they get paid 78% of what men do. (See section of Women's Rights).
- At Public colleges and universities, tuition should be free – this would help in the best of investments – that of human capital, and improve the quality of our population!
- Expand Social Security and lift the cap on taxable income to above $ 250,000. Fight attempts to reduce or privatize Social Security – it is a government operated pension program that people pay into during their working lives – it's not an entitlement!
- Guarantee healthcare for all as a right of citizenship – better health leads to a better quality and more productive population. But it should also be a right (see above section of Healthcare)
- Require employers to provide at least 12 weeks of paid family and medical leave , more vacation and more sick days. Taking care of family is important for the nation!
- We should enact universal childcare and pre-kindergarten program. Development specialists have said that 95% of brain development occurs before the age of 3 years.

- We need to strengthen unionizing rights by supporting unions for the passing of the Employee Free Choice Act. Directly empower those who work! In this manual we think that blue collar and white-collar employees should be represented on the company Boards. Also, employees should be increasing financed to be shareholder/owners and hence participate in management and ownership of the companies (two sentence added here).
- We need Wall Street Reform to avoid another Financial Crisis like 2008! The big financial institutions need to be divided into smaller units, so that no one of them can cause a crisis of the financial system. These companies are about 80% bigger than they were at the time of the crisis! (See section on Financial System Reform).

CONCLUSION

This is not just the conclusion of this book but an urging to engage in the process of building a better vision of America and then working to make it happen. We have to learn from the lessons of the past, understand them, better understand our issues, realize the true nature of the dangers we face today, develop a better vision that endures for a long time, and then work very hard to make it happen.

■■

Made in the USA
Columbia, SC
01 August 2020

14292606R00085